CW00500674

A History of the Northamptonshire Police

Richard Cowley

Sutton Publishing

First published in the United Kingdom in 2008 by
Sutton Publishing, an imprint of The History Press Limited
Cirencester Road · Chalford · Stroud · Gloucestershire · GL6 8PE

British Library Cataloguing in Publication Data
A catalogue record for this book is available from the British Library.

ISBN 978 0 7509 4956 9

Typesetting and origination by
The History Press Limited.
Printed and bound in England.

CONTENTS

The present-day helmet badge, in use since 1974, together with the badges of the three main constituent parts that make up today's Northamptonshire Police: Northampton Borough Police (1835–1966); Northamptonshire County Constabulary (1840–1966); and Northampton and County Constabulary (1966–1974). Can anyone spot the spelling mistake in the left-hand badge that caused a few red faces? *(Northamptonshire Police Museum)*

FOREWORD

Northamptonshire Police has a proud history stretching back over nearly 170 years. During that time the Force has experienced constant change and development, all of which has shaped the organisation we are today.

Those who were responsible for the origins of the Force could not have foreseen what policing in the twenty-first century would look like or the demands that would be made on us. Conversely, as we look back on our history through the pages of this book, it is difficult for us to imagine what policing was really like as the decades rolled by. These photographs from the Northamptonshire Police collection help us to trace our history and reflect on the way things have changed. I hope you enjoy this fascinating journey through time.

Peter F. Maddison, QPM
Chief Constable, Northamptonshire Police

INTRODUCTION

Organised modern police forces just didn't appear out of nowhere. There had to be a period of development leading up to the system of maintaining law and order which we now call 'policing'. In Great Britain, organised police forces are a relatively modern development, being only about 180 years old, which, in historical terms, is trifling.

National police development is complex, and to give a full description here would give the reader mental indigestion. So a *very* brief listing of the main points follow.

In 1829, the Metropolitan Police was started in London, and introduced a revolutionary concept into British policing, which was the full-time, paid, professional police officer – men whose only source of income and whose only job was to be a police officer – in complete contrast to the part-time unpaid amateurs of the previous, old parish constable system.

The year 1835 saw the introduction of the Municipal Corporations Act. This established Town Councils and Watch Committees, enabling them to form police forces for their boroughs, along the lines of the Metropolitan Police. In Northamptonshire, there were three boroughs affected: Northampton, Daventry and Higham Ferrers. Northampton and Daventry acted straight away and formed forces, but Higham Ferrers was harder to pin down.

The County Police Act was introduced in 1839. This gave county magistrates the power to form police forces for their counties if they so wished. But because of political pressure, the Act was not compulsory. Northamptonshire, however, was most progressive, and set up its force in January 1840.

The year 1856 saw the introduction of the County and Borough Police Act, which made police forces compulsory. It also established the Inspectorate of Constabulary which inspected each force annually. If considered efficient, then 50 per cent of yearly expenses would be paid by central government.

The introduction of the Local Government Act in 1888 took county administration out of the hands of the hereditary magistrates, and placed it firmly with politically elected County Councils. Consequently, police financial control passed into the hands of the Standing Joint Committee. The Act also put an end to the tiny borough police forces, which meant that Daventry Borough Police ceased to exist.

The Police Act was introduced in 1964. This gave the Home Secretary powers to make compulsory amalgamations of police forces. Northampton Borough Police was thus forced to amalgamate with Northamptonshire County Constabulary in 1966, to form the Northampton and County Constabulary.

The introduction of the Local Government Act in 1974 reformed local government and gave one police force per county. It was at this time that the Force name changed to Northamptonshire Police.

1

The Northampton Borough Police 1835–1966

Joseph Ball (1836–1851) was the automatic choice to become the first Chief Constable of the Northampton Borough 'new police' when it was formed in 1835 (under the Municipal Corporations Act), having been the 'Head Constable' of the old borough watchmen for the previous seven years. He was pensioned by the Watch Committee in October 1850, aged 67, but remained in post until his successor, Henry Keenan, took over in April 1851. Known affectionately as 'Old Joe Ball', this photograph was taken during his retirement. He died on 22 May 1877, aged 94. *(Northamptonshire Police Museum)*

PC9, James Stow, in the original uniform of the Northampton Borough Police (1835–1851); a blue 'swallow tail' coat with nine buttons, matching trousers and an 'S' buckle belt. The top hat was reinforced for protection, but could also be used to stand on to see over tall fences! The officer's identification number was in the lace decoration on the collar, and was therefore known as a 'collar number'. It copied the uniform of the Metropolitan Police, which itself was styled on the fashion of the day to emphasize that the police were a civilian, not military, force. *(Northamptonshire Police Museum)*

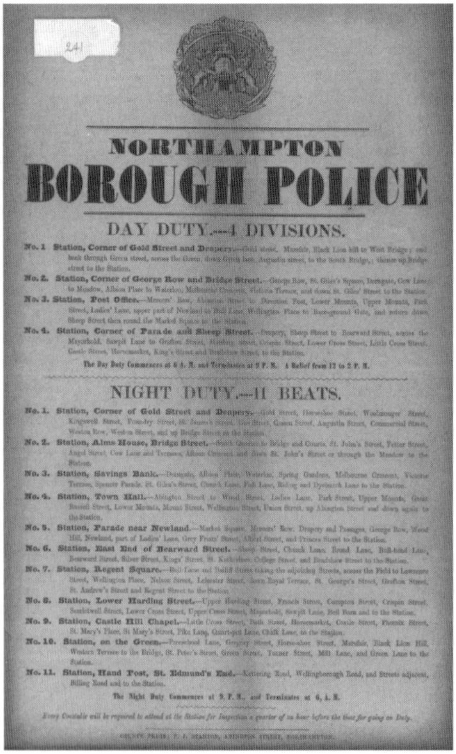

NORTHAMPTON

BOROUGH POLICE

DAY DUTY.—4 DIVISIONS.

No. 1 Station, Corner of Gold Street and Drapery.—[illegible]

No. 2. Station, Corner of George Row and Bridge Street.—[illegible]

No. 3. Station, Post Office.—[illegible]

No. 4. Station, Corner of Parade and Sheep Street.—[illegible]

The Day Duty Commences at 6 A. M. and Terminates at 7 P. M. A Relief from 12 to 2 P. M.

NIGHT DUTY.—11 BEATS.

No. 1. Station, Corner of Gold Street and Drapery.—[illegible]

No. 2. Station, Alms House, Bridge Street.—[illegible]

No. 3. Station, Savings Bank.—[illegible]

No. 4. Station, Town Hall.—[illegible]

No. 5. Station, Parade near Newland.—[illegible]

No. 6. Station, East End of Bearward Street.—[illegible]

No. 7. Station, Regent Square.—[illegible]

No. 8. Station, Lower Harding Street.—[illegible]

No. 9. Station, Castle Hill Chapel.—[illegible]

No. 10. Station, on the Green.—[illegible]

No. 11. Station, Hand Post, St. Edmund's End.—[illegible]

The Night Duty Commences at 9 P. M., and Terminates at 6, A. M.

Every Constable will be required to attend at the Station for Inspection a quarter of an hour before the time for going on Duty.

Following suggestions by Alderman Barwell of the Watch Committee, the original beats (the area patrolled by one constable) were reformed in 1849, to the ones on this poster. These new beats were on a rota, so that every constable walked every beat. Note that the constables on day duty had a thirteen-hour day – every day – with no days off; policemen had to wait until the Police (Weekly Rest Day) Act of 1910 to be granted one day off per week. The first police station was in Dychurch Lane, but moved to Fish Street in 1845. *(Northamptonshire Police Museum)*

Taking over in April 1851, Henry Keenan (1851–1887) was the second Chief Constable of the Northampton Borough Police. Born in Ireland in 1822, he had been in the Manchester City Police before coming to Northampton at the age of 29, making him one of the youngest Chief Constables in British history. He married a Northampton woman, Jane, but they had no children. He retired in 1887, and remained in Northampton until his death in October 1901. He is buried in Billing Road cemetery. *(Northamptonshire Police Museum)*

PC25, Walter Neeve. Walter Neeve joined the Northampton Borough Police on 14 January 1859, but was dismissed for being 'drunk when on duty at 3.18 a.m.' on 28 March 1860. In 1851, because the swallow tail coat had gone out of fashion, Henry Keenan, the new Chief Constable introduced the frock coat with nine buttons. By now, the belt had a large buckle upon which was engraved a crown. The officer's collar number consisted of metal figures and the reinforced top hat remained. *(Northamptonshire Police Museum)*

Borough police officers, mid to late 1850s. The frock coat with nine buttons is clearly seen, together with the top hats. Henry Keenan stands in the centre, together with his wife Jane, and a young man who is believed to be his nephew. The identities of the two men in plain clothes are unknown; however they were not detectives, as the Northampton Borough Police did not have its first detective officer until James Kemp in 1866. *(Northamptonshire Police Museum)*

Birmingham man James Kemp joined the Birmingham City Police before transferring to Northampton, where he became the Borough's first Detective Constable. At 10.30 p.m. on Boxing Day 1868, Kemp was walking across Campbell Square, Northampton, when he saw a drunken William Bridgewater with a shotgun. Kemp was shot in the shoulder at point blank range, and died in agony three days later. Although charged with murder, Bridgewater had his sentence reduced to manslaughter because he thought Kemp 'was my brother coming for me.' Kemp, as a detective, had been wearing plain clothes. James Kemp was the first Borough police officer to die on duty and was buried at Billing Road cemetery. *(Author's Collection)*

The Northampton Leather Trades' Exhibition, 1873. By this time, the helmet had replaced the top hat, but the rest of the uniform remained the same. The Long Service Chevron had been introduced – the first chevron was awarded after fourteen years' service, and was worn with the point uppermost on the right cuff. Subsequent chevrons were then awarded at five yearly intervals. The 'duty armlet' was also introduced at this time – this was worn on the left cuff to indicate that the officer was actually 'on duty'. It was originally made up of blue and white horizontal stripes, but this was later changed to blue and white vertical stripes. *(Northamptonshire Police Museum)*

The third Chief Constable of the Borough, Frederick Henry Mardlin (1887–1923) was a Bedfordshire man from a police family, his father having been a Sergeant. Joining the Bedfordshire force on his nineteenth birthday, he remained only three years before transferring to the Newcastle upon Tyne City Police, where he immediately joined the Criminal Investigation Department. Transferring again to Leicester Borough Police in 1881, he was soon promoted to Detective Inspector. Elected as Chief Constable of Northampton in October 1887, he remained until his retirement in 1923. He died in Northampton in 1931. *(Northamptonshire Police Museum)*

This photograph is believed to be of the Golden Jubilee of 1887. Official Police Jubilee medals were not issued to provincial forces, so provincial authorities promptly issued their own, Northampton included. It is thought this trio were the three longest serving officers of the force at the time this photograph was taken. The two outer officers are wearing three Long Service Chevrons, pointing upwards, denoting between twenty-four and twenty-nine years' service. After twenty-nine years' service, rather than wearing a fourth chevron, the three existing chevrons were turned to point downwards, as worn by the officer in the centre. *(Northamptonshire Police Museum)*

POLICE NOTICE.

CAUTION TO BICYCLISTS

By the Local Government Act of 1888, BICYCLES, TRICYCLES, VELOCIPEDES, and other similar Machines, are declared to be Carriages within the meaning of the Act of 1835, and any person furiously riding or driving the same is made liable to a Penalty of **FORTY SHILLINGS.**

The Local Government Act further provides that riders of such Machines, shall, between one hour after sunset, and one hour before sunrise, carry a LAMP attached to such Machine, and further, that such rider shall before overtaking any Carriage or Passenger give notice c his approach.

The Police have received strict instructions to enforce the provisions of the above-mentioned enactment.

F. H. MARDLIN,
CHIEF CONSTABLE.

Chief Constable's Office,
Town Hall, Northampton,

This police notice from 1888, warning that 'any person furiously riding or driving' a bicycle, tricycle or velocipede shall be fined 40*s*, reminds us of more principled times than today. *(Northamptonshire Police Museum)*

COUNTY BOROUGH of NORTHAMPTON.

POLICE INFORMATION.

LET OUT on HIRE.

ON THE 24th of OCTOBER, 1893,

And not since returned, "supposed stolen,"

A "WULFRUNA,"

SAFETY BICYCLE

Pneumatic Tyres, Rubbers burnt on side of Tyres, 30 inch Wheels, Tangent Spokes, Roller Chain, Oval Bottom Tubes, Scorcher Saddle, Ball Bearings throughout, Plated Parts, Maker, Barrett, Wolverhampton, second-hand.

To a man of the following description, who gave the name of GEORGE WILLIAMS, 10, Campbell Street, "false," about 20 years of age, 5 feet 5 or 6 inches, light hair and slight moustache, of respectable appearance.

Please cause enquiries to be made at Cycle Dealers, Pawnbrokers, and all likely places, with a view to the recovery of the Bicycle.

Any information obtained, please communicate with—

F. H. MARDLIN,

Chief Constable.

Sadly, we have become so inured to lawlessness that the theft of a bicycle today would elicit little or no response, let alone a full-scale poster campaign such as this one from October 1893. *(Northamptonshire Police Museum)*

COUNTY

BOROUGH OF NORTHAMPTON.

Police Information.

WANTED ON WARRANT charged with obtaining a Wallet, Calendar, Clock, Leather Blotting Case, Writing Album, Diary, various Books, Christmas Cards, Work Box, Safety Ink Bottle in Leather Case, Pens, Pencils, and other Stationery articles (not recovered) by means of false pretences, on the 16th December, 1893,

A JAPANESE giving the name of

P. T. TANNAKER,

alias Mitchko, about 35 years of age, 5-ft. high, medium build, dark swarthy complexion, small dark eyes, black hair, clean shaven, dressed in dark clothes, may be wearing a plaid waterproof coat with cape (which he also obtained by fraud from another tradesman), and a brown cap.

This man has been representing himself as the son of Tannaker who formerly had a travelling company of Artistes, and has thus obtained goods from various persons in this Borough. He may have letters addressed to him at the "Era" Office, London. Supposed to have had 3 months for fraud at Dewsbury recently.

Please cause immediate enquiries to be made, and if found arrest, and wire to

F. H. MARDLIN,

30th December, 1893. CHIEF CONSTABLE.

H. BERRILL, Printer, Abington Street, Northampton.

These notices were the only means of broadcasting information before the days of radio, television and the telephone. Some, like this one from December 1893, were kept within the borough, but others were sent to surrounding police forces, and in some cases to the Metropolitan Police in London. Whether 'P.T. Tannaker' was ever caught is unfortunately not known. *(Northamptonshire Police Museum)*

When Frederick Mardlin was elected Chief Constable in 1887, he demanded better facilities, so a new headquarters was built in Dychurch Lane next to the Guildhall. Officially opened in March 1892, this photograph was the first to be taken of the new premises. By the 1880s, the frock coat had been replaced by the short tunic, with eight buttons, but still with no pockets; and a different style of helmet had been adopted. The gentleman wearing the top hat on the left is unknown, but may have been the Chairman of the Watch Committee. *(Northamptonshire Police Museum)*

In 1900, the Borough of Northampton was enlarged by taking in the outlying districts, thus giving a population of 92,000. Policing from the central station in Dychurch Lane thus became impractical, and four suburban 'outstations' were established: in Far Cotton, Saint James, Kingsthorpe, and the Racecourse. This was the Far Cotton outstation in Euston Road. Frederick Mardlin, in common with most big towns, had organised a Borough Police Fire Brigade in 1888. Thus, until 1941 when the fire brigades were nationalised into the National Fire Service, the Borough Police were responsible for both policing and fire fighting. *(Northamptonshire Police Museum)*

Right: Sergeant Wooding, 1901. Although still in use for constables, Sergeants did not wear the Long Service Chevrons; but the armlet still remained. A St John Ambulance Brigade First Aid Efficiency badge was now worn on the upper right arm (Northampton being one of the national centres of the St John Ambulance Brigade upon its formation in 1888). Note the different helmet badge from the one seen in the photograph at the top of page 14; the badge changed when Queen Victoria died in 1901. *(Northamptonshire Police Museum)*

Below: PC Horace Laughton riding an early motorcycle. The date of this photograph is not known, but it must have been just prior to the First World War, judging by the helmet plate. *(Northamptonshire Police Museum)*

COUNTY BOROUGH OF NORTHAMPTON.

NOTICE

TO

KEEPERS OF PIGEONS.

No Person shall, in the United Kingdom, keep or have in his possession any CARRIER OR HOMING PIGEONS, unless he has obtained from the Chief Officer of Police of the District a Permit for the purpose (which Permit may at any time be revoked), and the Chief Officer of Police, may, if he considers it necessary or expedient to do so, cause any pigeons kept in contravention of this Regulation to be liberated.

These steps are taken in pursuance of the King's Proclamation and the Acts passed by Parliament for the defence of the Realm.

Application should at once be made for a Permit by any Person to whom this Order refers, to the Central Police Station, Dychurch Lane.

For non-compliance with this Regulation a person is liable to be arrested without a warrant and tried by Court Martial.

F. H. MARDLIN,
CHIEF CONSTABLE.

Central Police Station,
Northampton,
2nd November, 1914.

Above: A combined St John Ambulance Brigade (SJAB) exercise in the summer of 1915. The men are standing before an SJAB ambulance and an SJAB member is seen at the top right. An officer of the County Constabulary is standing second from the right in the back row, with a smaller badge on his helmet. The Deputy Chief Constable of the County, Superintendent William Hooper, is seated second from the right in the middle row, wearing the ribbon of the King's Police Medal, awarded to him in the New Year's Honours of 1915. On his left is Superintendent William Joiner, the Deputy Chief Constable of the Borough Police from 1913 until 1920. *(Northamptonshire Police Museum)*

Left: The fear of communication with the enemy by pigeon post was very real during the First World War, hence this poster from November 1914. *(Northamptonshire Police Museum)*

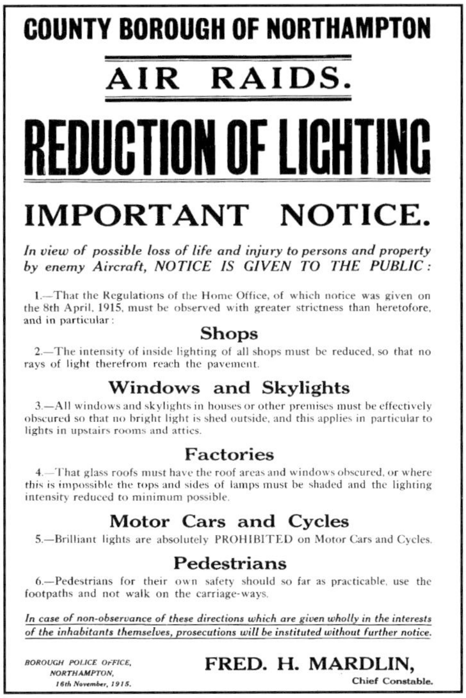

COUNTY BOROUGH OF NORTHAMPTON

AIR RAIDS.

REDUCTION OF LIGHTING

IMPORTANT NOTICE.

In view of possible loss of life and injury to persons and property by enemy Aircraft, NOTICE IS GIVEN TO THE PUBLIC:

1.—That the Regulations of the Home Office, of which notice was given on the 8th April, 1915, must be observed with greater strictness than heretofore, and in particular:

Shops

2.—The intensity of inside lighting of all shops must be reduced, so that no rays of light therefrom reach the pavement.

Windows and Skylights

3.—All windows and skylights in houses or other premises must be effectively obscured so that no bright light is shed outside, and this applies in particular to lights in upstairs rooms and attics.

Factories

4.—That glass roofs must have the roof areas and windows obscured, or where this is impossible the tops and sides of lamps must be shaded and the lighting intensity reduced to minimum possible.

Motor Cars and Cycles

5.—Brilliant lights are absolutely PROHIBITED on Motor Cars and Cycles.

Pedestrians

6.—Pedestrians for their own safety should so far as practicable, use the footpaths and not walk on the carriage-ways.

In case of non-observance of these directions which are given wholly in the interests of the inhabitants themselves, prosecutions will be instituted without further notice.

BOROUGH POLICE OFFICE,
NORTHAMPTON,
16th November, 1915.

FRED. H. MARDLIN,
Chief Constable.

The fear of air raids was also prevalent. On the morning of Friday 19 October 1917, thirteen Zeppelins took off from Germany to bomb 'middle England'. At 10.45 p.m., Zeppelin L45, commanded by Kapitänleutnant Waldemar Kolle, found itself over Northampton. Aiming for Northampton Castle railway station, Kolle dropped nine fire bombs. Bomb number five hit 46 Parkwood Street. Mrs Eliza Gammons was killed instantly, and her 13-year-old twin daughters, Gladys and Lily, were so badly burned that they died soon afterwards. *(Northamptonshire Police Museum)*

Northampton Borough Special Constabulary Transport Car, *c.* 1916. The Special Constabulary was a valuable source of manpower during the First World War – as it would be again during the Second World War. The officer standing to the left is Harry Barber, who was Special Commandant between 1916 and 1921. He was made a Member of the Order of the British Empire (MBE) in 1921 for his war work. *(Northamptonshire Police Museum)*

Victory roll call of the Northampton Borough Special Constabulary, *c.* 1920. One hundred and forty-two Special Constables are photographed here. Seated in the centre is Chief Constable Fred Mardlin, wearing his King's Police Medal awarded to him in the 1920 New Year's Honours. To his left is Commandant Harry Barber; and to his right is Sub-Commandant William Pepper Cross, who was made an Officer of the Order of the British Empire (OBE) in 1921. It is interesting to note that although all the officers are wearing the duty armlet, some have vertical stripes and some have horizontal stripes. *(Northamptonshire Police Museum)*

The first policewoman in the country was probably Miss Edith Watson, who was a member of the Women Police Volunteers organised by Miss Margaret Damer-Dawson in London in September 1914. Northampton Borough was quick to realise the potential of women police officers (unlike their county colleagues who waited until 1946), and enrolled Miss Helen King and Miss Eleanor Goodman as WPCs at a Watch Committee meeting in September 1918. In December 1918, Miss Margaret Scharina and Miss Mabel Farrier were also enrolled. This photograph is believed to show one of those four ladies. *(Northamptonshire Police Museum)*

John Williamson was the fourth Chief Constable of the Northampton Borough Police. A Westmorland man, John Williamson joined the Newcastle upon Tyne City Police in 1910. Transferring to the Huddersfield Borough Police in 1918, he was promoted to Chief Inspector within three years. He came to Northampton on 1 January 1924 at the age of 34, and was to remain for thirty-one years, retiring in 1955. This picture was taken in 1936, following his award of the OBE in the New Year's Honours. *(Northamptonshire Police Museum)*

John Williamson was awarded the King's Police Medal (KPM) in 1943, and promoted to Commander of the Order of the British Empire (CBE) as a result of his being a member of the Police Recruiting Mission to Palestine in 1948. His younger son, Frank, eventually became Chief Constable of Carlisle City Police, and later Cumbria Constabulary, before being appointed as Inspector of Constabulary. *(Northamptonshire Police Museum)*

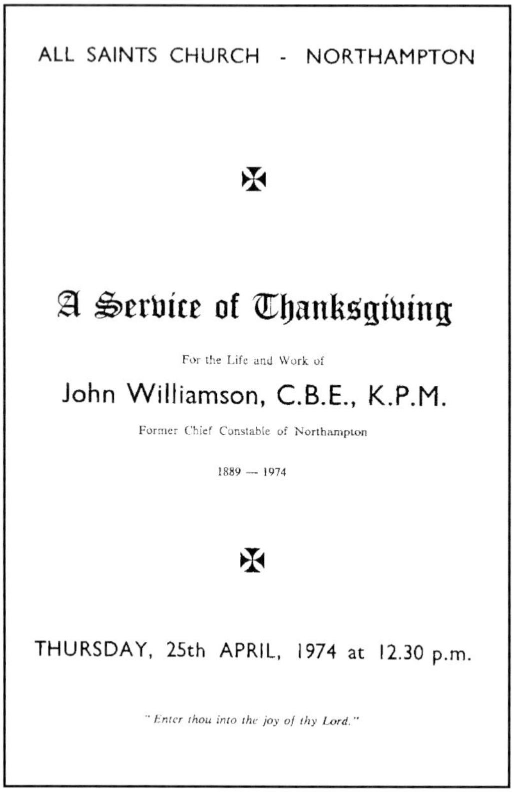

ALL SAINTS CHURCH - NORTHAMPTON

A Service of Thanksgiving

For the Life and Work of

John Williamson, C.B.E., K.P.M.

Former Chief Constable of Northampton

1889 — 1974

THURSDAY, 25th APRIL, 1974 at 12.30 p.m.

"Enter thou into the joy of thy Lord."

Left: John Williamson remained in Northampton after his retirement and died in April 1974. His memorial service included a tribute from Mr Harry Ambler OBE, QPM, the Chief Constable of Bradford City Police between 1957 and 1973. *(Northamptonshire Police Museum)*

Below: Northampton Borough Police cricket team, 1925. Seated in the centre (in the trilby hat) is Superintendent Peter Thompson, Deputy Chief Constable between 1920 and 1933. The rank of Superintendent/Deputy Chief Constable was created in 1913 when it was realised that the Chief Constable needed help with administrative work. The first Superintendent of the Borough was William Joiner (see top of page 16), who retired in 1920. *(Northamptonshire Police Museum)*

Although the General Strike proper only lasted for eight days – until 12 May 1926 – the mineworkers went on strike for the rest of the year, and there was much unrest in the coal mining areas of the country. The government thus sent squads of men from almost every police force in the country to the trouble spots. Northampton Borough Police sent a contingent of twenty-nine men to Hucknall Colliery, Nottinghamshire, where they stayed for about a month. *(Northamptonshire Police Museum)*

Hucknall Colliery in 1926: a good example of inter-force cooperation. The Northampton Borough officers are pictured on the left, a contingent of Northamptonshire County officers are on the right, and between them is a contingent from the Leeds City Police, with their large-badged 'cock's-comb' helmets. *(Northamptonshire Police Museum)*

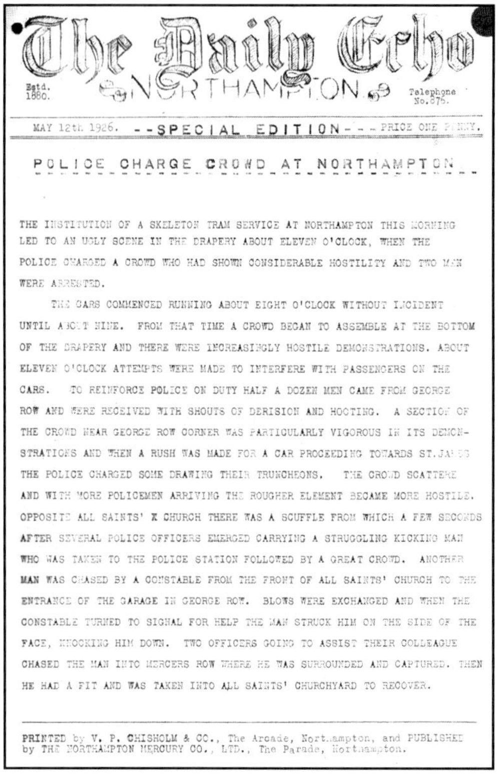

The Daily Echo
NORTHAMPTON

Estd. 1880. Telephone No. 875.

MAY 12th 1926. --SPECIAL EDITION--- PRICE ONE PENNY.

POLICE CHARGE CROWD AT NORTHAMPTON

THE INSTITUTION OF A SKELETON TRAM SERVICE AT NORTHAMPTON THIS MORNING LED TO AN UGLY SCENE IN THE DRAPERY ABOUT ELEVEN O'CLOCK, WHEN THE POLICE CHARGED A CROWD WHO HAD SHOWN CONSIDERABLE HOSTILITY AND TWO MEN WERE ARRESTED.

THE CARS COMMENCED RUNNING ABOUT EIGHT O'CLOCK WITHOUT INCIDENT UNTIL ABOUT NINE. FROM THAT TIME A CROWD BEGAN TO ASSEMBLE AT THE BOTTOM OF THE DRAPERY AND THERE WERE INCREASINGLY HOSTILE DEMONSTRATIONS. ABOUT ELEVEN O'CLOCK ATTEMPTS WERE MADE TO INTERFERE WITH PASSENGERS ON THE CARS. TO REINFORCE POLICE ON DUTY HALF A DOZEN MEN CAME FROM GEORGE ROW AND WERE RECEIVED WITH SHOUTS OF DERISION AND HOOTING. A SECTION OF THE CROWD NEAR GEORGE ROW CORNER WAS PARTICULARLY VIGOROUS IN ITS DEMONSTRATIONS AND WHEN A RUSH WAS MADE FOR A CAR PROCEEDING TOWARDS ST.JAMES THE POLICE CHARGED SOME DRAWING THEIR TRUNCHEONS. THE CROWD SCATTERED AND WITH MORE POLICEMEN ARRIVING THE ROUGHER ELEMENT BECAME MORE HOSTILE. OPPOSITE ALL SAINTS' X CHURCH THERE WAS A SCUFFLE FROM WHICH A FEW SECONDS AFTER SEVERAL POLICE OFFICERS EMERGED CARRYING A STRUGGLING KICKING MAN WHO WAS TAKEN TO THE POLICE STATION FOLLOWED BY A GREAT CROWD. ANOTHER MAN WAS CHASED BY A CONSTABLE FROM THE FRONT OF ALL SAINTS' CHURCH TO THE ENTRANCE OF THE GARAGE IN GEORGE ROW. BLOWS WERE EXCHANGED AND WHEN THE CONSTABLE TURNED TO SIGNAL FOR HELP THE MAN STRUCK HIM ON THE SIDE OF THE FACE, KNOCKING HIM DOWN. TWO OFFICERS GOING TO ASSIST THEIR COLLEAGUE CHASED THE MAN INTO MERCERS ROW WHERE HE WAS SURROUNDED AND CAPTURED. THEN HE HAD A FIT AND WAS TAKEN INTO ALL SAINTS' CHURCHYARD TO RECOVER.

PRINTED by V. P. CHISHOLM & CO., The Arcade, Northampton, and PUBLISHED by THE NORTHAMPTON MERCURY CO., LTD., The Parade, Northampton.

Left: The General Strike lasted for eight days, during which time, because printers were on strike, no newspapers were published. Newspaper owners (in this case the well known Dicey family, who had been publishing newspapers in Northampton for 200 years) tried to maintain some semblance of normality by publishing emergency editions in any format they could. *The Daily Echo* was published by the *Northampton Mercury*, and this edition of 12 May 1926, the last day of the strike, reports the mayhem and bad feeling caused by the strike. *(Northamptonshire Police Museum)*

Below: Northampton Borough Police football team – winners of the 1927/28 season Northampton Rotary Club Cup. Seated in the front row to the left of the cup is Chief Constable John Williamson, and to the right is Superintendent Peter Thompson. *(Northamptonshire Police Museum)*

Above: The Swimming Section of Northampton Borough Police Athletic Club, 1928. PC John Taylor Cookson (standing third from the right) became Deputy Chief Constable between 1953 and 1964. *(Northamptonshire Police Museum)*

Right: PC Victor Eales was awarded the silver medal of the Society for the Protection of Life from Fire for his rescue of two elderly people from a first floor flat in Wellingborough Road at 1 a.m. on 30 November 1928. Alerted by a passing couple, PC Eales went to the scene and found that the elderly couple were both deaf and dumb, and could not be woken by throwing things at their window. Breaking in, he groped his way up the smoke filled stairs, and brought the couple out in two separate journeys. PC Eales' medal can be seen in the Police Museum. *(Northamptonshire Police Museum)*

Because Northampton was one of the original national St John Ambulance centres, the Marquess of Northampton gave the city a silver cup in 1902, which became the premier trophy for First Aid competitions in the county. The Northampton Borough Police First Aid Team won the trophy in 1931, the first time in twenty-nine years that a non-St John Ambulance Brigade team had won the trophy. The Chief Constable, John Williamson, Deputy Chief Constable Peter Thompson, and Inspector Denney are shown seated with the team. Standing from left to right: PC89 Symonds, PC122 Jones, PC128 Stone and PS20 Spence. *(Northamptonshire Police Museum)*

The Road Traffic Act of 1930 introduced the Highway Code as well as placing the responsibility for road traffic regulation fairly and squarely onto the shoulders of the police. In response, all forces introduced specialist traffic departments. Because large cars were not suitable for Northampton's narrow town streets, the first Borough motor patrols were motorcycle/sidecar combinations. This is the only surviving photograph of a rider in uniform, PC Ernie Jones, seen here in the early 1930s. *(Northamptonshire Police Museum)*

The sidecar combinations were used by the Criminal Investigation Department as well. Detective Constables Bishop and Allen set out to make enquiries in Northampton in 1930. *(Northamptonshire Police Museum)*

In 1932, two BSA three-wheeled cars replaced motorcycles as the main form of motor patrol vehicles. They were so successful that they covered 52,000 miles during their first year, and had to be replaced annually. PC Elston is driving this car in 1935. *(Northamptonshire Police Museum)*

With the advent of larger fire engines, the Northampton Borough Police Fire Brigade moved to a central garage in Dychurch Lane. This Dennis fire engine is seen being called out in about 1930. *(Northamptonshire Police Museum)*

The Northampton Borough Male Voice Choir, 1932. This was the last picture taken of the Deputy Chief Constable, Superintendent Peter Thompson (seated fifth from the left in the front row), before his retirement. Seated third from the right in the front row is PC Hedley Jeffcott, who, as a Sergeant in 1938, was awarded the King's Police Medal (KPM) for Gallantry (as opposed to Meritorious Service), for the rescue of two men from a gas-filled sewer, the only man of either force to be so decorated. He received his decoration personally from the King. Since 1954, the Queen's Police Medal for Gallantry has only been awarded posthumously. *(Northamptonshire Police Museum)*

The Northampton Borough Police Football Club, winners of the Northampton Rotary Cup and the Bedfordshire County Police Cup in the 1932/33 season. Seated on the right is Superintendent William Afford, the new Deputy Chief Constable. While in the army during the First World War, he was awarded the Distinguished Conduct Medal. Despite applying for Chief Constableships in other forces, William Afford remained at Northampton until his retirement in 1953. In 1949 he was awarded the KPM, two years after his brother, Ebenezer, had been awarded the same decoration (as Deputy Chief Constable of the Huntingdonshire County Constabulary), making them the only brothers to hold the KPM simultaneously. *(Northamptonshire Police Museum)*

John Williamson introduced police boxes in the mid-1920s. These were located in numerous locations throughout the borough and were, in effect, mini police stations. If no officer was present, telephone communication to central headquarters could be made by the public. This photograph shows PC Cockcroft making a call in 1925. *(Northamptonshire Police Museum)*

Police pillars were introduced in 1932. These were for use by both the police and the public as they contained a telephone which was linked to central headquarters. The telephone was activated by opening the door, behind which was a handset and loudspeaker. The light on the top flashed to attract the attention of the local beat bobby when there was a message for him. *(Northamptonshire Police Museum)*

By the 1960s these pillars were gradually being phased out as private telephones and police personal radios came upon the scene. *(Northamptonshire Police Museum)*

A police rally was held in Hyde Park, London, for the Silver Jubilee of King George V in 1935. Contingents from every police force in the land took part. This is the contingent of the Northampton Borough Police. Seated on the right is PC Victor Eales, wearing his medal from the Society for the Protection of Life from Fire. Because it was presented by a private society and not the monarch, it was worn on the right side, not the left, as were the official medals (all First World War medals) worn by the others. *(Northamptonshire Police Museum)*

Motor patrols, late 1930s. The three-wheelers were abandoned for bigger and more powerful vehicles, as shown by the two cars on the left with their uniform patrol officers. The smaller car is the plain-clothes CID vehicle, for the use of the two detective officers. *(Northamptonshire Police Museum)*

Dychurch Lane, Northampton, in 1940, during its last days as the Borough Police Headquarters. Superintendent Afford is standing before the main gate, which is decked out in wartime bomb damage precautions. Built in 1892, by the mid-1920s, the facilities were looking decidedly dated. Several government inspectors had commented unfavourably, which resulted in the withholding of the Certificate of Efficiency in 1928, meaning the loss of the Exchequer Grant of 50 per cent of annual costs from central government. Negotiations were therefore quickly started for new accommodation, which would eventually result in the building of Campbell Square. *(Northamptonshire Police Museum)*

Looking east along Dychurch Lane. The building on the left is the McRae bacon-curing warehouse – scene of the infamous McRae murder. Andrew McRae had left his wife and family in Birmingham, and brought Annie Pritchard and their baby daughter to Northampton. On the night of 20 July 1892, McRae murdered Annie and the baby in the warehouse, using the copper employed for curing the bacon to boil down the baby's body. But he could only boil down Annie's head and arms, so he dumped her torso in a sack in the village of East Haddon. McRae was hanged in January 1893. *(Northamptonshire Police Museum)*

The main gate in Dychurch Lane, with blue light hanging from the archway. The Northampton Borough coat of arms can be seen above the archway. *(Northamptonshire Police Museum)*

The doorway to the Women Police Department, Dychurch Lane. This was only moved to Dychurch Lane in 1940. Previously, the department had been housed in Guildhall Police Box, in Guildhall Road, to keep the women away from the male police officers, it was said – or vice versa. *(Northamptonshire Police Museum)*

Left: The courtyard at the rear of the main gate, Dychurch Lane. Note the rubble guards against the doors and the sandbags at the window, which is quite clearly where the upper photograph on page 14 was taken forty-eight years previously. *(Northamptonshire Police Museum)*

Below: Inspectors Ryder and Rudkin in the Inspectors' room, Dychurch Lane police station. *(Northamptonshire Police Museum)*

Sergeant A. Allen and PC C. Jenkins in the general office at Dychurch Lane police station. Note the officers are in full uniform, even when they worked permanently indoors. 'Shirt sleeve order', of shirt and epaulettes worn without a jacket, did not arrive for another twenty years. *(Northamptonshire Police Museum)*

The Criminal Investigation Department office, Dychurch Lane, July 1941. Note the bound copies of the *Police Gazette* on the bookshelf. These were circulated by the Metropolitan Police to all other forces, giving details and photographs of criminals and their activities. It is still published today. *(Northamptonshire Police Museum)*

Left: The switchboard at Dychurch Lane. As well as being a 9-to-5 administrative headquarters, Dychurch Lane was also a twenty-four-hour police station. Telephone traffic would thus have been continuously round the clock, not only from members of the public, but also from beat officers telephoning in. *(Northamptonshire Police Museum)*

Below: The 'salubrious' canteen in Dychurch Lane. It is to be wondered if today's police officers would put up with such accommodation. The calendar is dated November 1941 – just one month before the move to Campbell Square. *(Northamptonshire Police Museum)*

The parade room, Dychurch Lane. Officers had to parade fifteen minutes before the start of their shift to receive and give information. Note the wartime 'Tin Hats' on the pegs rather than the familiar helmets. Note also the capes. The cape was the best piece of the uniform that was issued, far warmer than an overcoat, and allowing all kinds of things to be carried underneath it (thermos flasks, sandwiches, etc.) without being detected. The capes ceased being issued in the 1970s. *(Northamptonshire Police Museum)*

The constables' report writing room, Dychurch Lane. Note the canvas bunk beds in case emergency accommodation was required. These headquarters were demolished to make room for the new Guildhall extension, built in the same style as the 'Gothic Revival' Northampton Guildhall by Edward Godwin in 1864. Unfortunately, the Dychurch Lane Police Headquarters of 1892 never came near to matching the Guildhall. *(Northamptonshire Police Museum)*

In August 1938, the competition for the design of a new police station was won by J.C. Prestwich & Sons of Leigh, Lancashire. This is the architect's drawing of the new design. Nikolaus Pevsner in his *Buildings of England: Northamptonshire*, calls the design 'desperately uninspired'. *(Northamptonshire Police Museum)*

The Borough Gaol had stood on this site in Campbell Square since 1845; prior to that it had been located in Fish Street. The Fish Street premises – on the site of what is now the Subway Sandwich Bar – then became the Borough Police Headquarters. The Borough Gaol was closed in 1922 and was sold to the Town Council for £14,268 in 1929 as the ideal site for the new police headquarters. Demolition of the 3½-acre site began a year later. *(Northamptonshire Police Museum)*

The whole complex (police station, fire station, courts and swimming pool) was built by Glenn & Sons Ltd for a quotation of £72,995, although the final total was £90,000. The new police station was being erected while the old gaol was being demolished. The last parts to go were the front walls, seen in this photograph. *(Northamptonshire Police Museum)*

Campbell Square, ready to receive its new occupants. *(Northamptonshire Police Museum)*

The move from Dychurch Lane to Campbell Square began in December 1941, and was completed in a short time. Seated from left to right at Campbell Square's Enquiry Office are: Sergeant Green, Inspector May and Miss Goldsmith. *(Northamptonshire Police Museum)*

John Williamson (seated), with Superintendent Afford in his old office at Dychurch Lane. *(Northamptonshire Police Museum)*

Above: John Williamson with his secretary in his plush new office in Campbell Square. Note the photographs of his predecessors, Henry Keenan and Joseph Ball, on the far wall. In the cabinet on the far left can be seen a series of scrapbooks, into which were pasted every press cutting of relevance to the Borough Police. These continued until the end of the force in 1966, and are preserved in the Police Museum. *(Northamptonshire Police Museum)*

Right: WPC Wentworth and WPC Smith, of the Northampton Borough Police, near Holy Sepulchre Church, *c.* 1942. Note the change in style of uniform to one more in keeping with the fashion of the day. *(Northamptonshire Police Museum)*

During the early months of the Second World War, it was feared that air raids would obliterate the telephone and communication systems. In case this should happen, the Police Auxiliary Messenger Service (PAMS) was started, with young lads recruited to act as runners and messengers. In the event, of course, the air raids never happened, and the PAMS were disbanded soon afterwards. This is Cyril Mason in his PAMS uniform. *(Author's Collection)*

The wartime uniform of the Borough Police. This is PC Bill Stone in 1943. Note that there is no St John First Aid badge, duty armlet or belt, and the helmet has been replaced by the standard pattern British 'Tin Hat'. *(Northamptonshire Police Museum)*

Police recruitment ceased during the Second World War. Police manpower therefore came from three sources: the Special Constabulary; the First Police Reserve (recently retired policemen who had contracted to return to service in the event of war); and the War Reserve (men over the age of 30, who, although untrained, were contracted to serve as policemen for the duration). Northampton Borough Police operated two parts of the Special Constabulary: the Foot Section and the Mobile Section. This is the Mobile Section of Central Division in 1939 – note the jodhpurs and leggings. *(Northamptonshire Police Museum)*

The St James' Division of the Foot Section of the Northampton Borough Police Special Constabulary, 1940. Many of the men are wearing medals awarded during the First World War, which had finished twenty-two years earlier. *(Northamptonshire Police Museum)*

The Far Cotton Division of the Northampton Borough Special Constabulary Foot Section, September 1941. *(Northamptonshire Police Museum)*

Parade of Northampton Borough Police Mobile Specials, led by Special Chief Inspector George Norris MM, in 1942. They are marching up St Giles Square towards Derngate. Note the Barclay's Bank building in the background on the right, which is all that remains of the façade of the old County Gaol (as opposed to the Borough Gaol), built in 1846. Originally twice that length, to include a gateway and the Governor's house, part was demolished in 1881 when the gaol was closed and sold off (together with the County Constabulary Chief Constable's house next door) and this row of shops was built on the site. *(Northamptonshire Police Museum)*

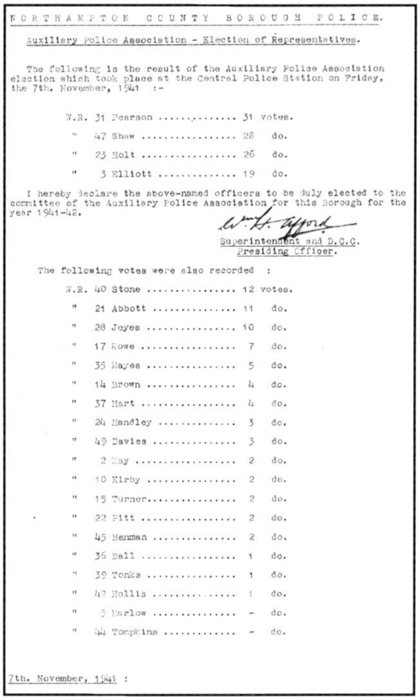

NORTHAMPTON COUNTY BOROUGH POLICE.

Auxiliary Police Association - Election of Representatives.

The following is the result of the Auxiliary Police Association election which took place at the Central Police Station on Friday, the 7th. November, 1941 :-

W.R.	31	Pearson	31	votes.
"	47	Shaw	28	do.
"	23	Holt	26	do.
"	3	Elliott	19	do.

I hereby declare the above-named officers to be duly elected to the committee of the Auxiliary Police Association for this Borough for the year 1941-42.

Wm H. Afford
Superintendent and D.C.C.
Presiding Officer.

The following votes were also recorded :

W.R.	40	Stone	12	votes.
"	21	Abbott	11	do.
"	28	Joyes	10	do.
"	17	Rowe	7	do.
"	35	Mayes	5	do.
"	14	Brown	4	do.
"	37	Hart	4	do.
"	24	Handley	3	do.
"	49	Davies	3	do.
"	2	Ray	2	do.
"	10	Kirby	2	do.
"	15	Turner................	2	do.
"	22	Pitt	2	do.
"	45	Henman	2	do.
"	36	Ball	1	do.
"	39	Tonks	1	do.
"	42	Hollis	1	do.
"	5	Harlow	-	do.
"	44	Tompkins	-	do.

7th. November, 1941 :

While the regular police officers had the Police Federation to represent them, the War Reserve Constables, not being trained police officers, had no representative body, so they formed their own. The Auxiliary Police Association for Northampton Borough was formed on 7 November 1941. This is the first page of the Minute Book, showing the selection of the steering committee. *(Northamptonshire Police Museum)*

John Williamson (centre front) and Superintendent Afford (with peaked cap) with part of the Northampton Civil Defence Corps and Air Raid Wardens, 1943. Standing to Mr Williamson's right is believed to be Alderman Arthur Ray, the Chairman of the Watch Committee until 1943, and this photograph was probably taken on his retirement. Behind Mr Williamson is John Taylor Cookson, who would succeed William Afford as Superintendent/Deputy Chief Constable in 1953. *(Northamptonshire Police Museum)*

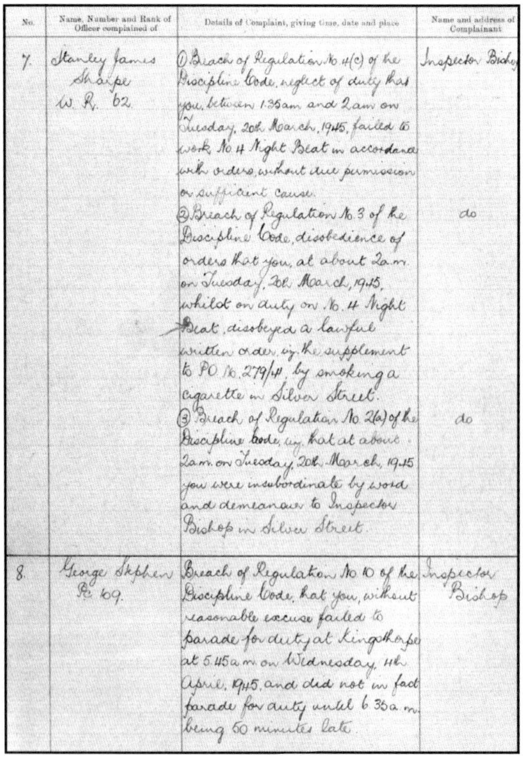

No.	Name, Number and Rank of Officer complained of	Details of Complaint, giving time, date and place	Name and address of Complainant
7.	Stanley James Sharpe W. R. 62	(1) Breach of Regulation No. 4(c) of the Discipline Code, neglect of duty that you, between 1.35am and 2am on Tuesday, 20th March, 1945, failed to work No 4 Night Beat in accordance with orders, without due permission or sufficient cause.	Inspector Bishop
		(2) Breach of Regulation No. 3 of the Discipline Code, disobedience of orders that you, at about 2a.m. on Tuesday, 20th March, 1945, whilst on duty on No. 4 Night Beat, disobeyed a lawful written order, viz. the supplement to PO No. 279/44, by smoking a cigarette in Silver Street.	do
		(3) Breach of Regulation No. 2(a) of the Discipline Code, viz. that at about 2am. on Tuesday, 20th March, 1945 you were insubordinate by word and demeanour to Inspector Bishop in Silver Street.	do
8.	George Stephen R. 69.	Breach of Regulation No 10 of the Discipline Code, that you, without reasonable excuse failed to parade for duty at Kingsthorpe at 5.45a.m. on Wednesday, 4th April, 1945, and did not in fact parade for duty until 6 35a.m. being 50 minutes late.	Inspector Bishop

Above: Despite the war, police administration continued as normal, with inspections by the Inspectorate of Constabulary to see if the police were being maintained in a state of efficiency. This is the Northampton Borough Police Bicycle Corps inspection of 1945. The Inspector is Sir Llewellyn Atcherley, who had retired in 1935 but had been recalled in 1939. This must have been one of his last inspections, as he would finally retire in 1945 at the age of 75. *(Northamptonshire Police Museum)*

Left: Although not as harsh as the previous century, nevertheless, by the end of the war, police discipline still instilled respect into the police officers. Even War Reserve Constables (untrained men, only serving for the duration) were not exempt. Consider this misdemeanour of March 1945, for which the War Reserve officer was fined £1 4*s* 3*d* and cautioned. *(Northamptonshire Police Museum)*

The royal visit of HRH the Princess Elizabeth, now HM the Queen, to Northampton in 1946. The parade is in front of the Guildhall, with All Saints Church in the background. John Williamson looks on. *(Northamptonshire Police Museum)*

The Traffic Department, late 1940s. This photograph was taken in the garages behind Campbell Square Headquarters. Note that the cars have no badges or markings, not even blue lights, which only came in with the introduction of the 'Panda Cars' nearly twenty years later. The large Commer van doubled as a rescue and general utility vehicle, as well as a Black Maria (used to transport prisoners). *(Northamptonshire Police Museum)*

Police recruitment resumed after the war, and some men returned to service, having been in the armed forces. These were some of the 1946 intake. Some of the men felt themselves unsuited to the role and resigned, while others continued until they reached their pension. *(Northamptonshire Police Museum)*

The Crown Court took over as the main higher criminal court in 1971, replacing the Quarter Sessions and the Assizes. Previously, the Assizes, nigh on 800 years old, were held two or three times a year before two High Court judges. The Judges' Parade through the streets of Northampton to attend a church service at All Saints Church, seen here, before the Assizes proper started, was one of the highlights of the year, and included marching bands. The parade was accompanied by a police escort. *(Northamptonshire Police Museum)*

Dennis Baker was the fifth and last Chief Constable of Northampton Borough Police. Born in Brighton in 1913, Baker joined the Brighton Borough Police and rose to the rank of Superintendent. After twenty-two years' service, he was chosen as the Chief Constable of Northampton in 1955. He was awarded the Queen's Police Medal for Meritorious Service in 1964. When the amalgamation of the Borough and County forces became known, Dennis Baker was offered the post of Deputy Chief Constable of the new force, under John Gott. He declined, and retired. He remained in Northampton, and died in February 2002. *(Northamptonshire Police Museum)*

The Criminal Investigation Department of the Northampton Borough Police in 1955, on the retirement of Detective Inspector Bishop (seated in the middle of the front row). On his left is Superintendent John Cookson, the Deputy Chief Constable. Standing on the extreme left is DC Tom Paintain, who eventually rose to become Chief Inspector. It was Tom Paintain who, during his last years of service in headquarters at Wootton Hall, started the Police Museum and Archive. It was his farsightedness in preserving and cataloguing photographs, documents and artefacts that made the compilation of this book possible. *(Northamptonshire Police Museum)*

Tom Paintain currently enjoys retired life in Weston Favell, where he produces paintings such as this one, now hanging in Wootton Hall. *(Northamptonshire Police Museum)*

PCs Fellows and Ferguson take delivery of new motorcycles, 1956. Motorcycles were deemed more practical round some of the narrow streets in Northampton town centre. Standing behind are, from left to right: Superintendent/Deputy Chief Constable John Cookson; Chief Inspector Bryan Tomblin, Traffic Department; Inspector Thomas Nicholson (who became Superintendent/Deputy Chief Constable between 1964 and 1966); Chief Constable Dennis Baker; and Alderman A. Lyne, Chairman of the Watch Committee. *(Northamptonshire Police Museum)*

Sergeant Pardo and PC Mayes take delivery of a Triumph Tiger and BSA Rocket in 1963. *(Northamptonshire Police Museum)*

The Northampton Borough Police Underwater Search Unit, 1961. The unit was kept on when the force amalgamated in 1966, and continued into the 1970s before being disbanded. Nowadays, if such a unit is required, those of neighbouring forces are called upon. *(Northamptonshire Police Museum)*

The same unit being inspected by HM Inspector of Constabulary, Joseph Manuel, at the penultimate yearly inspection of the force in 1965. Mr Sydney Strickland, the Chairman of the Borough Watch Committee (wearing spectacles), can be seen standing on the left. *(Northamptonshire Police Museum)*

The Control Room at Campbell Square, March 1965. The central telephone is the '999' telephone. Not only was this console equipped with the radio system of the Borough Police, but it had a receiver which monitored the County Constabulary radio transmissions as well. In fact, it was this point which was the essence of why the Home Secretary wanted the forces to amalgamate. 'What was the advantage' Chief Constable Dennis Baker was asked by the Counsel for the Home Secretary at the public enquiry, 'of having two force control rooms only two miles apart?' Dennis Baker was unable to answer. *(Northamptonshire Police Museum)*

Right: A public enquiry to hear objections against the amalgamation of the Borough Police and County Constabulary was held in December 1964. The recommendations were published in February 1965. The result was no surprise. The Home Secretary had long since made up his mind, and the amalgamation was going to go ahead anyway. The public enquiry had only been a sop for the Borough Police, and had just delayed the inevitable. The Home Secretary signed the amalgamation order, and the two forces were combined on 1 April 1966. Thus ended the Northampton Borough Police after 130 years of existence. *(Northamptonshire Police Museum and reproduced under the terms of the PSI Click-Use Licence (C2008000521))*

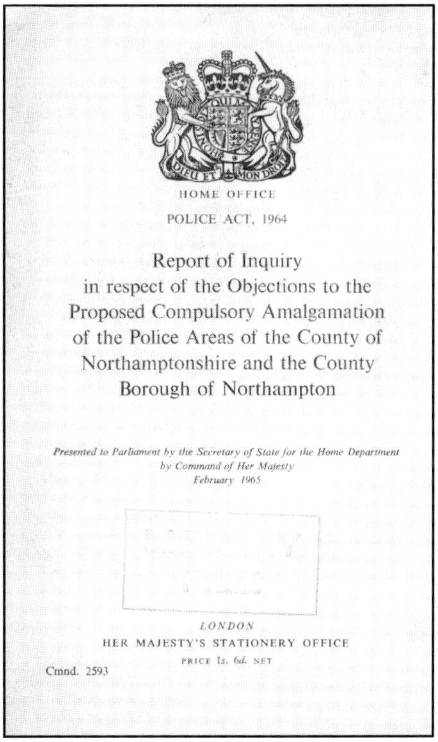

DIEU ET MON DROIT

HOME OFFICE

POLICE ACT, 1964

Report of Inquiry
in respect of the Objections to the
Proposed Compulsory Amalgamation
of the Police Areas of the County of
Northamptonshire and the County
Borough of Northampton

*Presented to Parliament by the Secretary of State for the Home Department
by Command of Her Majesty
February 1965*

LONDON
HER MAJESTY'S STATIONERY OFFICE
PRICE 1s. 6d. NET

Cmnd. 2593

Below: When it became clear that the force was no longer to exist separately, the inevitable reunions took place. This one, in early 1966, was between the Regular Old Comrades' Association and the Northampton Ex-Police War Reserve Association. Dennis Baker and Thomas Nicholson are seen standing fourth and sixth from the right. *(Northamptonshire Police Museum)*

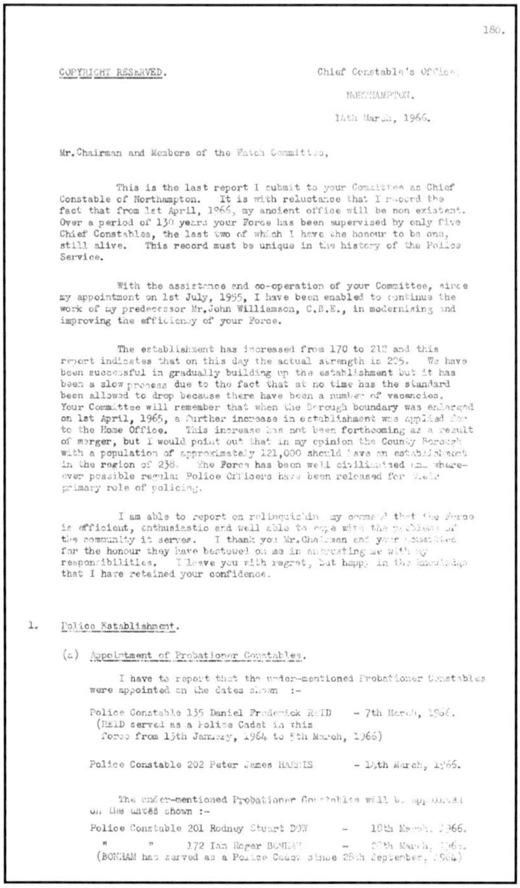

180.

COPYRIGHT RESERVED.

Chief Constable's Office,
NORTHAMPTON.
14th March, 1966.

Mr. Chairman and Members of the Watch Committee,

This is the last report I submit to your Committee as Chief Constable of Northampton. It is with reluctance that I record the fact that from 1st April, 1966, my ancient office will be non existent. Over a period of 130 years your Force has been supervised by only five Chief Constables, the last two of which I have the honour to be one, still alive. This record must be unique in the history of the Police Service.

With the assistance and co-operation of your Committee, since my appointment on 1st July, 1955, I have been enabled to continue the work of my predecessor Mr. John Williamson, C.B.E., in modernising and improving the efficiency of your Force.

The establishment has increased from 170 to 212 and this report indicates that on this day the actual strength is 205. We have been successful in gradually building up the establishment but it has been a slow process due to the fact that at no time has the standard been allowed to drop because there have been a number of vacancies. Your Committee will remember that when the Borough boundary was enlarged on 1st April, 1965, a further increase in establishment was applied for to the Home Office. This increase has not been forthcoming as a result of merger, but I would point out that in my opinion the County Borough with a population of approximately 121,000 should have an establishment in the region of 238. The Force has been well civilianised and wherever possible regular Police Officers have been released for their primary role of policing.

I am able to report on relinquishing my command that the Force is efficient, enthusiastic and well able to cope with the problems of the community it serves. I thank you Mr. Chairman and your Committee for the honour they have bestowed on me in entrusting me with my responsibilities. I leave you with regret, but happy in the knowledge that I have retained your confidence.

1. Police Establishment.

(a) Appointment of Probationer Constables.

I have to report that the under-mentioned Probationer Constables were appointed on the dates shown :-

Police Constable 135 Daniel Frederick REID - 7th March, 1966.
(REID served as a Police Cadet in this Force from 15th January, 1964 to 5th March, 1966)

Police Constable 202 Peter James HARRIS - 14th March, 1966.

The under-mentioned Probationer Constables will be appointed on the dates shown :-

Police Constable 201 Rodney Stuart DOW - 18th March, 1966.
" " 172 Ian Roger BONHAM - 28th March, 1966.
(BONHAM has served as a Police Cadet since 28th September, 1964)

Dennis Baker's last report to the Northampton Borough Watch Committee, dated 14 March 1966. Note that the very last constable to join the Northampton Borough Police was PC172 Ian Roger Bonham, sworn in only three days before the end of the force (see page 117). *(Northamptonshire Police Museum)*

To mark the passing of the force, the final Annual Report was a souvenir edition, containing the history of the force, a full list of every member – both police and civilian – and messages of appreciation from the Mayor and the Chairman of the Watch Committee. *(Northamptonshire Police Museum)*

2

Higham Ferrers Borough Police, 1836–1874 & Daventry Borough Police, 1836–1888

The Town Hall, Higham Ferrers. The Higham Ferrers Borough Police presents us with a mystery. The town was obliged to set up a force in 1835 under the Municipal Corporations Act, but nowhere can any trace of it be found. The Minutes of the Court of Common Council are preserved in the County Record Office, and record the annual appointment of two constables, but these are assumed to be the part-time parish constables, as there was no difference in the method of their election before or after 1836. There is certainly no mention of a Watch Committee or Chief Constable. *(Author's Collection)*

However, there is this photograph of John Blackwell Martin, 'Police Constable at Higham Ferrers', from 1860. His uniform is different to the County Constabulary of 1860 (see lower photograph on page 63). PC Martin has a crown and another badge on his collar, instead of just the collar number of a County constable. So is this a photograph of PC Martin of the Higham Ferrers Borough Police of 1860? In the County Constabulary records, an entry appears for a John B. Martin, joining in December 1858, and promoted to Sergeant in the Wellingborough Division in 1865, but no other details are given. The mystery remains. *(Author's collection)*

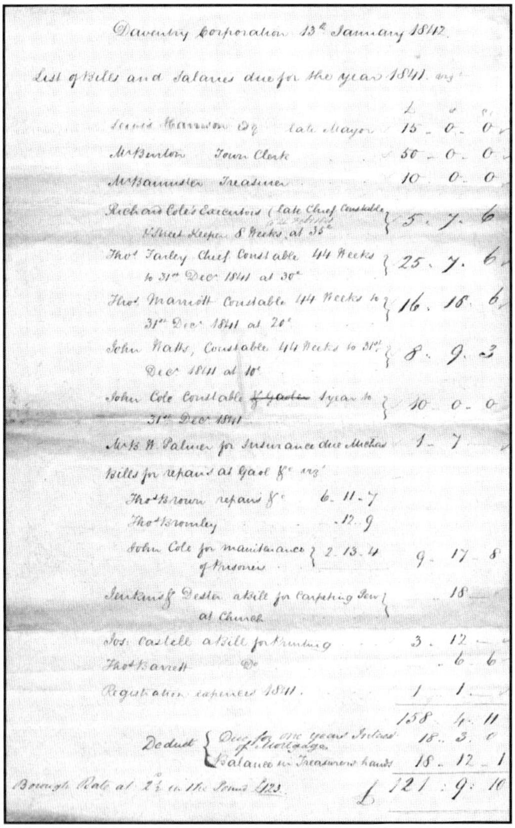

Daventry Corporation 13th January 1842.

List of Bills and Salaries due for the year 1841. viz

	£	s	d
Lewis Harrison Esq late Mayor	15	0	0
Mr Burton Town Clerk	50	0	0
Mr Bannister Treasurer	10	0	0
Richard Cole's Executors (late Chief Constable & Street Keeper 8 Weeks at 35s	5	7	6
Thos Farley Chief Constable 44 Weeks to 31st Decr 1841 at 30s	25	7	6
Thos Marriott Constable 44 Weeks to 31st Decr 1841 at 20s	16	18	6
John Watts, Constable 44 Weeks to 31st Decr 1841 at 10s	8	9	3
John Cole Constable 1 year to 31st Decr 1841	10	0	0
Mr B H Palmer for Insurance due Michas	1	7	
Bills for repairs at Gaol &c viz: Thos Brown repairs &c 6-11-7; Thos Bromley -12-9; John Cole for maintenance of Prisoners 2-13-4	9	17	8
Jenkins & Dester a Bill for Carpeting Pew at Church		18	
Jos. Castell a Bill for Printing	3	12	
Thos Barrett Do		6	6
Registration expenses 1841	1	1	
	158	4	11
Deduct: Due for one years Interest of Mortgage	18	3	0
Deduct: Balance in Treasurers hands	18	12	1
Borough Rate at 2d in the Pound £123	121	9	10

Daventry, however, did form a police force in 1835, but not much has survived. This is the list of salaries for the Daventry Corporation for 1842. It can be seen that Richard Coles, the Chief Constable, had died during the year, to be replaced by Thomas Farley. Three other police officers comprised the entire force: Thomas Marriott, John Watts and John Cole. *(Northamptonshire Police Museum)*

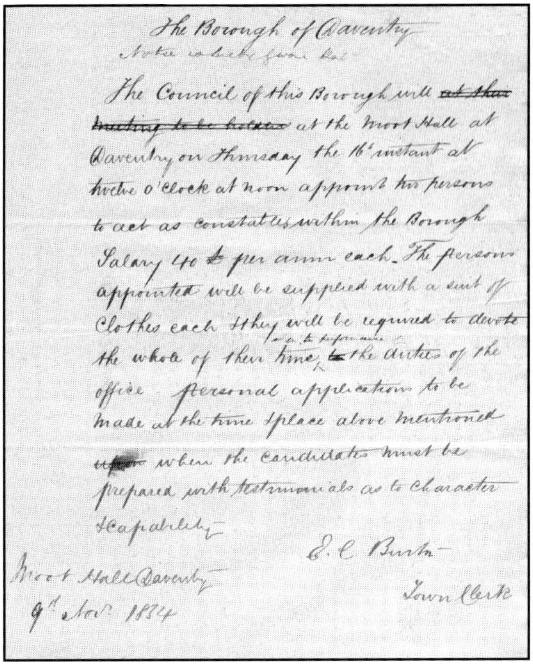

The Borough of Daventry
Notice is hereby given that

The Council of this Borough will ~~at their meeting to be holden~~ at the Moot Hall at Daventry on Thursday the 16th instant at twelve o'clock at noon appoint two persons to act as constables within the Borough Salary 40 £ per annm each. The persons appointed will be supplied with a suit of Clothes each & they will be required to devote the whole of their time and to the performance of the duties of the office personal application to be made at the time & place above mentioned ~~upon~~ when the candidates must be prepared with testimonials as to Character & Capability

E. C. Burton
Town Clerk

Moot Hall Daventry
9th Nov 1854

Judging by this draft copy of an advertisement destined for the *Northampton Mercury*, the number of police officers in the Daventry force had been reduced to two by 1854. *(Northamptonshire Police Museum)*

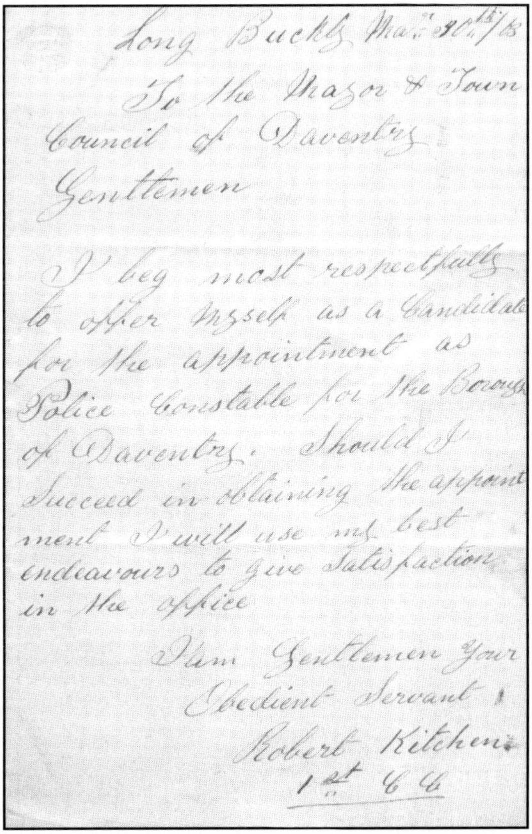

Long Buckby Mar 30th/18

To the Mayor & Town Council of Daventry

Gentlemen

I beg most respectfully to offer myself as a Candidate for the appointment as Police Constable for the Borough of Daventry. Should I succeed in obtaining the appointment I will use my best endeavours to give satisfaction in the office

I am Gentlemen Your
Obedient Servant
Robert Kitchen
1st C C

This reply is from another advertisement placed in the local press:

'To the Mayor and Town Council of Daventry Gentlemen I beg most respectfully to offer myself as a Candidate for the appointment as Police Constable for the Borough of Daventry. Should I succeed in obtaining the appointment I will use my best endeavours to give satisfaction in the office. I am, Gentlemen, Your Obedient Servant Robert Kitchen 1st C[lass] C[onstable].'

PC Kitchen was in the County Constabulary (see lower photograph on page 63). He did not get this job. *(Northamptonshire Police Museum)*

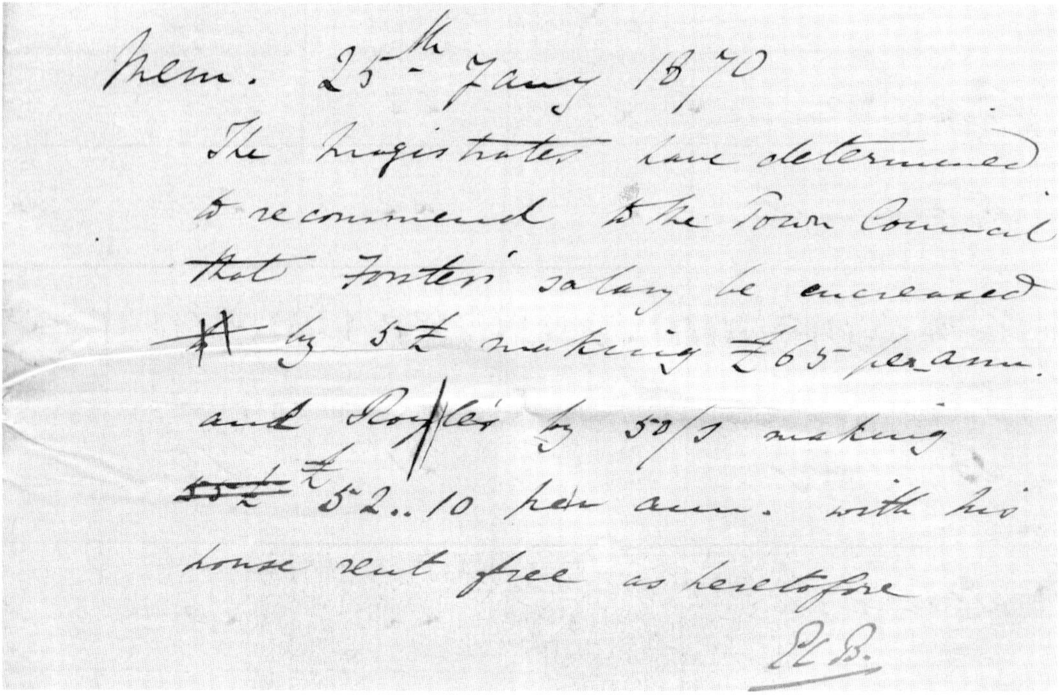
Mem. 25th Jany 1870
The Magistrates have determined
to recommend to the Town Council
that Foster's salary be increased
by 5£ making £65 per ann.
and Royle's by 50/s making
£52..10 per ann. with his
house rent free as heretofore
E.B.

Two officers seem to constitute the full strength of the Daventry Borough Police from here on. This memo from Edward Burton, the Town Clerk, to the magistrates of the Borough, is dated 25 January 1870, and reads, 'The Magistrates have determined to recommend to the Town Council that Foster's salary be increased by £5 making £65 per annum, and Royle's by 50/*s* making £52 10*s* per annum, with his house rent free as heretofore.' *(Northamptonshire Police Museum)*

The only set of Daventry Borough Police uniform buttons in existence. The buttons bear the name 'Daventry Police' and the date 1595, which is presumably the date of incorporation of the borough. The design is of a man standing with an axe and holding a tree, which apparently is supposed to represent a Dane cutting down a tree, which is a pun on Danetre, the old name of Daventry. *(Northamptonshire Police Museum)*

3

Northamptonshire County Constabulary, 1840–1966

Henry Goddard, first Chief Constable of the County Constabulary. Born in 1800, Londoner Henry Goddard joined the Bow Street Runners. When the Runners were disbanded in 1839, Goddard was snapped up by the Northamptonshire magistrates in May 1840. Goddard was a 'hands-on' policeman, not an administrator, and there is ample evidence to suggest he was not happy in Northamptonshire. And when ostensibly, he was injured on duty (no details of which remain), he used this as an excuse to leave, and returned to London as the door-keeper to the House of Lords in 1849. He died in 1883. *(Northamptonshire Police Museum)*

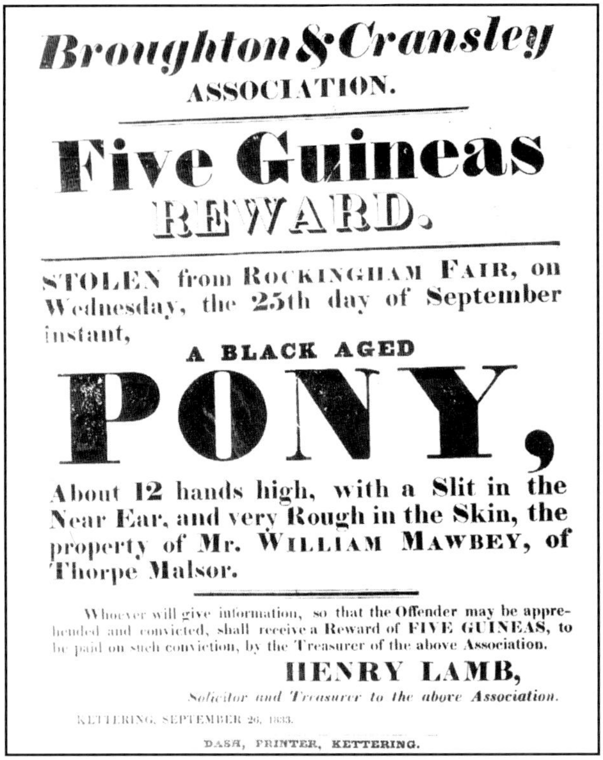

Broughton & Cransley
ASSOCIATION.

Five Guineas
REWARD.

STOLEN from ROCKINGHAM FAIR, on Wednesday, the 25th day of September instant,

A BLACK AGED
PONY,

About 12 hands high, with a Slit in the Near Ear, and very Rough in the Skin, the property of Mr. WILLIAM MAWBEY, of Thorpe Malsor.

Whoever will give information, so that the Offender may be apprehended and convicted, shall receive a Reward of FIVE GUINEAS, to be paid on such conviction, by the Treasurer of the above Association.

HENRY LAMB,
Solicitor and Treasurer to the above Association.

KETTERING, SEPTEMBER 26, 1833.

DASH, PRINTER, KETTERING.

Poster from the Broughton and Cransley Association offering a five guinea reward for the return of a pony. During the eighteenth and nineteenth centuries (before organised police forces were introduced), plaintiffs at court had to pay their own expenses, which could be ruinous. To get over this, people who had something worth losing banded together in Associations and paid an annual fee into a central pool, so that if they needed to go to court, then the court expenses would be paid from this central pool. The Associations also offered the service of poster campaigns throughout the district in the event of a crime being committed against any of its members. There were thirty-three such Associations in Northamptonshire. *(Northamptonshire Police Museum)*

Rowell Association.

2 GUINEAS
REWARD.

WHEREAS some evil disposed Person or Persons did, on MONDAY NIGHT last, maliciously cut off and carry away

THE HAIR
FROM THE TAILS OF FOUR
BLACK CART HORSES,

being in a Field in the Lordship of *Orton*, the Property of Mr. WILLIAM TONGUE, of *Rowell*.

Whoever will give Information so that the Offender or Offenders, may be Apprehended and Convicted, shall receive a Reward of ONE GUINEA, to be paid by the Treasurer of the above Association; and a further Reward of ONE GUINEA, will be paid by the said WILLIAM TONGUE.

HENRY LAMB,
SOLICITOR AND TREASURER.

KETTERING, J[illegible] 8th, 181[illegible]

[illegible] PRINTER, KETTERING

Poster from the Rowell (Rothwell) Association. Note the reward: two guineas in 1819 would have been about a month's wages for a farm worker (equivalent to about £900 at today's value). With the coming of the full-time constabularies, court cases cost the victim nothing, so the Associations quickly declined. Some still exist today, although more as dining clubs than crime fighting organisations. *(Northamptonshire Police Museum)*

Above: St Giles Square, Northampton. The County Constabulary Headquarters (left) and Chief Constable's house (right) were used from 1846 until 1881. The small porch in between the two buildings was built in 1877. Previously, rooms had been hired, but in 1846 a new County Gaol and Governor's House were built between Guildhall Road and St Giles Square. So the old County Gaol became the new County Constabulary Headquarters, which also provided the Chief Constable's house. These buildings were sold in 1881, and the County Headquarters moved to George Row. *(Author's Collection)*

Right: Henry Lambart Bayly became the second Chief Constable in 1849, though sadly no photograph of him has survived. Unlike Goddard, Bayly was a born administrator, having been in the Honourable East India Company and the Irish Constabulary. He immediately rearranged the force. Instead of seven divisions under the supervision of a Superintendent, each division was now under the newly introduced rank of Inspector, with a Superintendent in charge of a district of two or more divisions. This new Book of Rules and Regulations was issued to every officer. Bayly retired to Kent in 1875. He died in 1886 aged 77. *(Northamptonshire Police Museum)*

RULES AND REGULATIONS

FOR THE GOVERNMENT AND GUIDANCE OF THE

NORTHAMPTONSHIRE
COUNTY CONSTABULARY,

(Under the Act 2 & 3 Vict., chap. 93.)

AS APPROVED OF BY
THE JUSTICES IN QUARTER SESSIONS,
ON THE 10TH DAY OF APRIL, 1850.

BY H. L. BAYLY,
CHIEF CONSTABLE.

NORTHAMPTON: PRINTED BY JAS. BUTTERFIELD.
1850.

Brackley Divisional Police Station and Magistrates' Court. Bayly persuaded the magistrates to start a programme of purpose-built divisional police stations. The first three, Brackley, Towcester and Kettering, were all built between 1851 and 1854, at a total cost of £2,500. Of these, only Brackley survives, and is now a private dwelling. *(Author's Collection)*

Kettering Divisional Police Station and Magistrates' Court, London Road, before the First World War. Originally comprising just the police station, built in 1852, the Magistrates' Court was added in 1905. Kettering Police Station and Magistrates' Court was finally demolished in 1968, to be replaced with the present building. *(Author's Collection)*

Above: The opening of Kettering Magistrates' Court, 1905. Why the police officers appear to be wearing white helmets is unknown. *(Author's Collection)*

Right: William Cartwright, the first Inspector of Constabulary, in 1856. Although not a policeman, Cartwright was appointed because of his enormous experience of local government. Coming from the well-known Northamptonshire family from Aynho, Cartwright was an army officer, and fought in the Peninsular campaign and at the Battle of Waterloo. He was the most influential of the first three Inspectors of Constabulary, but retired disillusioned in 1868, when he realised that central government was not implementing the police reforms that were needed. He died in 1873 and was buried at Aynho. *(Northamptonshire Record Office)*

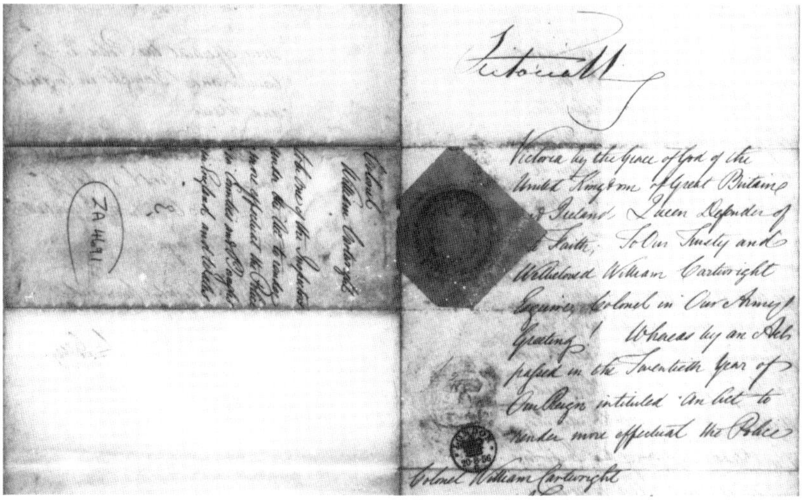
Victoria R

Victoria by the Grace of God of the United Kingdom of Great Britain & Ireland, Queen Defender of the Faith, To Our Trusty and Wellbeloved William Cartwright Esquire, Colonel in Our Army Greeting! Whereas by an Act passed in the Twentieth Year of Our Reign intituled "An Act to render more effectual the Police

Colonel William Cartwright

Colonel William Cartwright

to be one of the Inspectors under the Act to render more efficient the Police in Counties and Boroughs in England and Wales

ZA 4691

The County and Borough Police Act of 1856 made police forces compulsory, which they had not been before. The Act also established the Inspectorate of Constabulary whose job was to inspect every force annually, and if found efficient, then central government would pay 50 per cent of the annual costs. William Cartwright was the first Inspector to be appointed. Dated 1 August 1856, Cartwright's appointment warrant as HM Inspector of Constabulary is preserved at the Northamptonshire Record Office. *(Northamptonshire Record Office)*

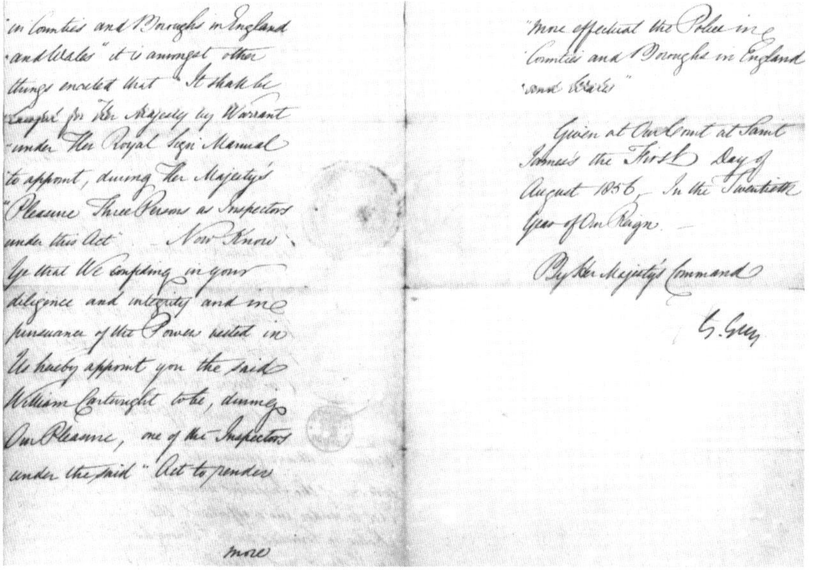
"in Counties and Boroughs in England and Wales" it is amongst other things enacted that "It shall be lawful for Her Majesty by Warrant under Her Royal Sign Manual to appoint, during Her Majesty's Pleasure Three Persons as Inspectors under this Act" Now Know Ye that We confiding in your diligence and integrity and in pursuance of the Powers vested in Us hereby appoint you the said William Cartwright to be, during Our Pleasure, one of the Inspectors under the said "Act to render

more

"more effectual the Police in Counties and Boroughs in England and Wales"

Given at Our Court at Saint James's the First Day of August 1856 In the Twentieth Year of Our Reign.

By Her Majesty's Command

G. Grey

'Victoria by the Grace of God of the United Kingdom of Great Britain & Ireland, Queen Defender of the Faith; To our Trusty and Well beloved William Cartwright Esquire, Colonel in Our Army Greeting! Whereas by an Act passed in the Twentieth Year of Our reign intitled 'An Act to render more efficient the Police in Counties and Boroughs in England and Wales' . . . It shall be lawful for her Majesty . . . to appoint . . . Three persons as Inspector . . . Now know ye that . . . in pursuance of the Powers vested in Us hereby appoint you the said William Cartwright to be . . . one of the Inspectors under the said Act'. *(Northamptonshire Record Office)*

RETURN SHEWING THE TOWNS AND VILLAGES AT PRESENT REQUIRING ADDITIONAL STRENGTH.

Division.	Places where extra Men are required.	Present Strength.	Extra force required.	Name of Town or Village proposed to be under additional Constable.	Population of each Parish.	Total Population.	Acres.
Brackley	Brackley	1 Constable	1 Constable	Brackley	2383	2908	7241
				Evenley	525		
Towcester	Towcester	1 Constable	1 Constable	Towcester	2715	2715	2790
	Shutlanger	—	1 Constable	Shutlanger	394	1115	5182
				Stoke Bruerne	430		
				Alderton	151		
				Easton Neston	140		
Daventry	Weedon	1 Sergeant	1 Constable	Weedon	2189	2780	4755
				Dodford	238		
				Stowe-Nine-Churches	353		
Northampton	Guilsborough	—	1 Sergeant	Guilsborough	990	1792	7092
				Thornby	252		
				Hollowell	....		
				Cold Ashby	446		
				Coton	104		
Wellingborough	Wellingborough	2 Constables	1 Sergeant, 1 Constable	Wellingborough	6382	6382	4490
Kettering	Kettering	2 Constables	1 Constable	Kettering	5845	5845	2849
	Grafton Underwood	—	1 Constable	Grafton Underwood	294	1361	8062
				Warkton	315		
				Barton Seagrave	199		
				Cranford	553		
Little Bowden	Weston by Welland	—	1 Constable	Weston	204	917	6528
				Ashley	348		
				Sutton Bassett	147		
				Dingley	111		
				Brampton Ash	107		
Oundle	Oundle	1 Constable	1 Sergeant	Oundle	3040	3040	5306
Thrapston	Thrapston	1 Constable	1 Constable	Thrapston	1257	1686	5629
				Denford	429		
	Lowick	—	1 Constable	Lowick	427	1375	5151
				Islip	627		
				Sudborough	321		

13 Sergeants and Constables
3 Reserve

Total 16

(COPY.)

To the Clerk of the Peace of the County of Northampton.

SIR,—We do hereby give you Notice that we shall, at the General Quarter Sessions of the Peace for the County of Northampton, to be holden at Northampton, on Wednesday, the Nineteenth day of October now next ensuing, at One o'clock in the Afternoon, move the Court that the Police Force of the said County be increased by the addition of Sixteen Constables.

Dated this 18th day of June, One thousand eight hundred and sixty-four.

(Signed) GEORGE ASHBY ASHBY
THOS. STEELE
H. M. STOCKDALE
W. MACKWORTH DOLBEN
W. GRANT.

The Inspectorate of Constabulary did not have the power to implement changes to police forces, only powers to recommend, which the county magistrates and borough Watch Committees could either implement or ignore as they wished. This is a recommendation from Cartwright for an increase in the Northamptonshire County Constabulary, dated 1864. Cartwright found that central government was not willing to give the Inspectorate coercive powers, thus his disillusionment when he retired, four years after this memo – which was not acted upon. *(Northamptonshire Police Museum)*

PC Robert Kitchen, 1860. This is the oldest photograph of a county police officer in uniform. The original uniform (of which no photograph has survived) was a ten-buttoned single-breasted blue coat, grey trousers and a plain black top hat. A leather belt containing cases for handcuffs and a staff (truncheon) was worn. By 1860, the uniform had changed to a knee length, eight-buttoned frock coat with no pockets, and the same colour trousers. Although not shown, the belt and accessories would still have been worn. Collar numbers were metal. The helmet was a 'bowler' type, with a metal badge. *(Author's Collection)*

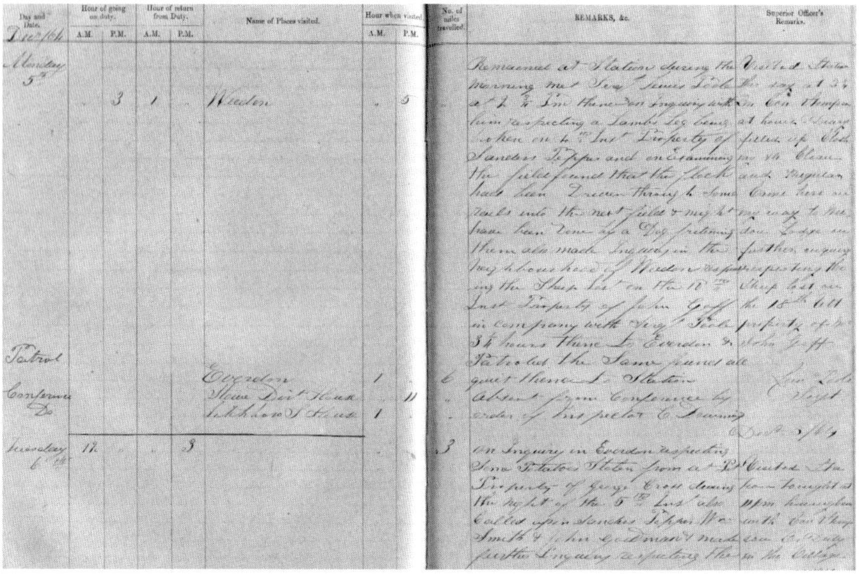

Three pages from the diary of PC Richard Stimpson, dated Monday 5 December to Friday 9 December 1864. PC Stimpson was 28-years-old and stationed on the Everdon beat. Being a country beat, his duties mainly consisted of agricultural problems (sheep worrying, theft of livestock etc.), plus the inevitable supervision of local beer houses to cater to the Victorians' paranoia about drink and the working classes, which also gave the very real risk of being assaulted by the local drunks. *(Northamptonshire Police Museum)*

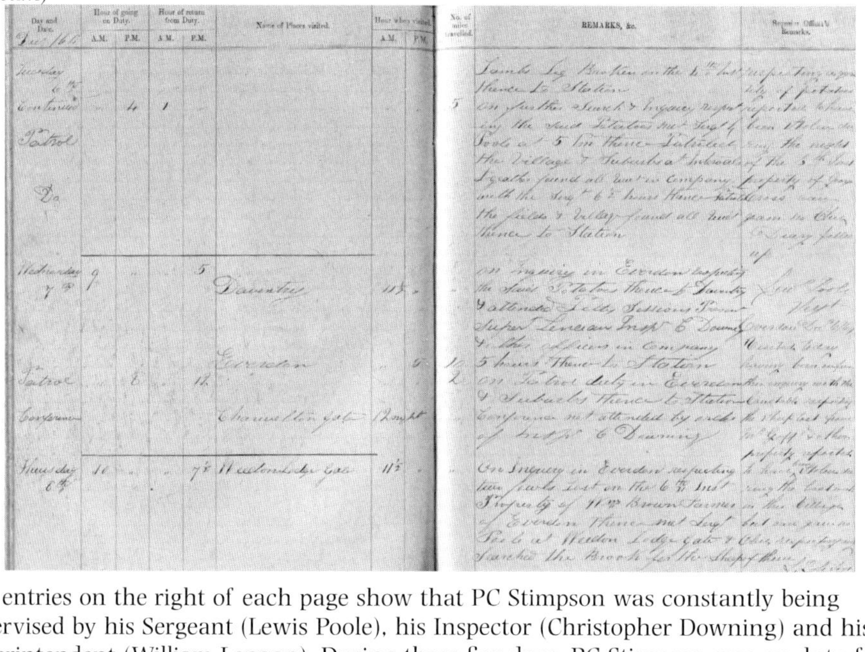

The entries on the right of each page show that PC Stimpson was constantly being supervised by his Sergeant (Lewis Poole), his Inspector (Christopher Downing) and his Superintendent (William Lenaan). During these five days, PC Stimpson was on duty for seventy-one hours, and walked forty-five miles. Amazingly, he did this every day of the year, with no time off. Police officers did not get days off until the Police (Weekly Rest Day) Act of 1910 came into force. *(Northamptonshire Police Museum)*

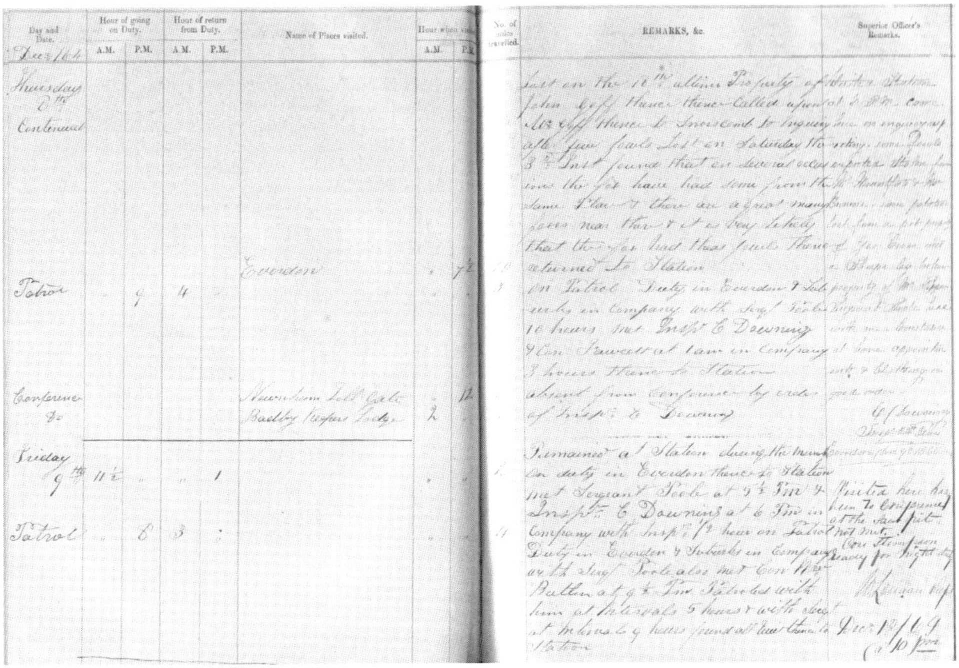

Given the harsh discipline and working conditions, is it any wonder that the turnover of manpower was so high? PC Stimpson resigned in May 1865. *(Northamptonshire Police Museum)*

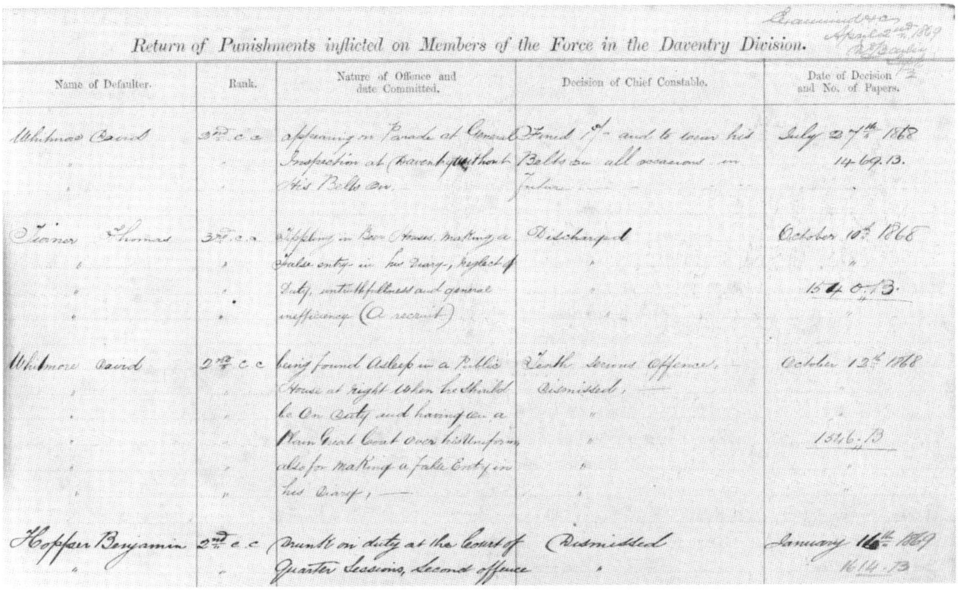

Return of Punishments inflicted on Members of the Force in the Daventry Division.

Name of Defaulter.	Rank.	Nature of Offence and date Committed.	Decision of Chief Constable.	Date of Decision and No. of Papers.
Whitmore David	3rd c.c	appearing on Parade at General Inspection at Daventry without His Belts on.	Fined 1/- and to wear his Belts on all occasions in future	July 27th 1868 1469.13.
Turner Thomas	3rd c.c	Tippling in Beer Houses, making a false entry in his diary, neglect of duty, untruthfulness and general inefficiency (a recruit)	Discharged	October 10th 1868 1540.13.
Whitmore David	2nd c.c	being found Asleep in a Public House at night when he should be on duty and having on a Plain Great Coat over his uniform, also for making a false entry in his diary, —	Tenth serious offence. Dismissed.	October 12th 1868 1546.13
Hopper Benjamin	2nd c.c	Drunk on duty at the Court of Quarter Sessions, Second offence	Dismissed	January 16th 1869 1614.13

The Daventry Division Punishment Book for 1868. In four months, three constables had been dismissed for drinking on duty. Implemented by Henry Bayly in 1868, Punishment Books were kept at the Divisional Headquarters stations for ease of reference. These books lasted until the Second World War, when punishments were then entered onto individual officers' personal records. *(Northamptonshire Police Museum)*

In 1870, the County Constabulary started photographing criminals and recording them in a book. Unfortunately, only one book has survived, dating from 1870 to 1871. The photographs provide a glimpse of the dress of the ordinary people of the time. This page shows six convicted thieves from 1870–71. *(Northamptonshire Police Museum)*

The divisions were reorganised in 1860 and two more were added: Thrapston and Little Bowden. This is the Thrapston Divisional Police Headquarters and Magistrates' Court, completed in late 1860. Today, it survives as a hotel; the Court House Inn. The Little Bowden Divisional Headquarters were completed in 1864. However, by the Local Government Act of 1888, Little Bowden was taken over by Leicestershire, and so the beats in the division were absorbed into the Kettering Division. Little Bowden police station survives as a private dwelling. *(Author's Collection)*

A snow covered Oundle Divisional Headquarters and Magistrates' Court, January 1985. Oundle was the last Divisional Headquarters to be built in the first phase of the building programme started by Bayly in 1851. Completed in 1877, Oundle station still survives as local government offices. The new Oundle police station in Glapthorn Road was built in 1977. *(Author's Collection)*

Charles Pearson, the 'Three Hour Chief Constable'. When Henry Bayly retired as Chief Constable in 1875 and the position was advertised, an incredible 143 candidates applied. A shortlist was drawn up for the magistrates. Charles Pearson, the Chief Constable of Caernarfonshire, was chosen. Inspecting his new house, he was evidenlty unimpressed, and returned to the magistrates to request new accommodation. Despite attempts at compromise, Pearson promptly resigned after just three hours in the post, making him the shortest serving Chief Constable of all time. *(Caernarfonshire Record Office)*

After the Pearson fiasco, the second choice, Thomas Orde Hastings Lees, was appointed. Like Bayly, Lees was from the Irish landed gentry. After taking an MA in law at Trinity College, Dublin, Lees was called to the Bar. Because the Royal Irish Constabulary operated a commission system, Lees was commissioned in December 1868 as a Cadet Officer, serving for seven years before being chosen as the Chief Constable of Northamptonshire in October 1875. He would resign in a fit of pique in 1881, after the Chief Constable's house in St Giles Square was sold from under him without his knowledge (see pages 59 and 71). *(Northamptonshire Police Museum)*

CODE

OF

RULES AND REGULATIONS

FOR THE

NORTHAMPTONSHIRE CONSTABULARY

APPROVED BY

THE COURT OF QUARTER SESSIONS,

April, 1881;

ISSUED BY

THE CHIEF CONSTABLE,

October, 1881.

NORTHAMPTON:

STANTON AND SON, PRINTERS, ABINGTON STREET.

During his tenure, Lees reissued the much-enlarged Code of Rules and Regulations, originally published by Bayly in 1850. Although returning to the Bar, he (unsuccessfully) contested the Parliamentary seat of Northampton in 1886. In 1890, Lees was elected as the first Chief Constable of the newly formed Isle of Wight County Constabulary. He personally received the Diamond Jubilee medal from Queen Victoria at Osborn House, for his handling of the island's Jubilee celebrations. He resigned in 1899 and retired at the age of 53. He lived at Guilsborough, where his wife came from, and died there in 1924. *(Northamptonshire Police Museum)*

Part of the Wellingborough town strength, *c*. 1876. Note the different style of helmet, and the pouch on the belt. It is believed that this was an experimental type of helmet, which never proved popular and was quickly abandoned in favour of the kepi style patrol cap, and the more conventional helmet of a few years later. *(Northamptonshire Police Museum)*

Left: The headstone of Superintendent Lewis Poole, London Road cemetery, Wellingborough. The inscription reads: 'To the memory of Lewis Poole who was killed in a railway accident near Northampton on the night of October 18 1877, aged 40 years. He had been a member of the Northamptonshire Constabulary for upwards of twenty years & was at the time of his death Superintendent of the Wellingborough District. This stone is erected by the members of the force as a mark of their esteem and as a token of their sympathy with his widow and family . . .' *(Author's Collection)*

Below: The Great Houghton train crash on Thursday 18 October 1877 claimed the lives of four people, three of them policemen. A ballast train was in a head-on collision with a passenger train when an inexperienced signalman allowed both trains to run along the same line in opposite directions. As a result, Superintendent Poole, Sergeant Isaac Wilson, PC Thomas Barrett, and a newspaper reporter, Thomas Leatherland, all received fatal injuries. The signalman and his supervisor were both found not guilty of manslaughter at the Northamptonshire Assizes in March 1878. *(Author's Collection)*

The Wellingborough town strength, *c.* 1877. The constable seated in the front row fourth from the right is PC John Brown. He joined in March 1875 at the age of 20 and went to Wellingborough, where he would have known Superintendent Lewis Poole for two and a half years. *If*, judging by the foliage on the wall behind, this photograph was taken in early spring, and *if* John Brown doesn't look more than 23, then there is the distinct possibility that the officer standing on the extreme left of the middle row, with the moustache, is Superintendent Lewis Poole himself. *(Northamptonshire Police Museum)*

The Sessions House and County Hall, George Row, Northampton, from a pre-First World War postcard. In 1881, because the County Gaol became obsolete, the whole complex, including the Chief Constable's house and County Constabulary Headquarters, were sold off without the knowledge of Thomas Lees, the Chief Constable. So, at a stroke he not only lost his headquarters, but his home as well and resigned in a fit of pique. The new County Constabulary Headquarters then became George Row, where they were to remain until 1950, when the force moved to its present headquarters of Wootton Hall. *(Author's Collection)*

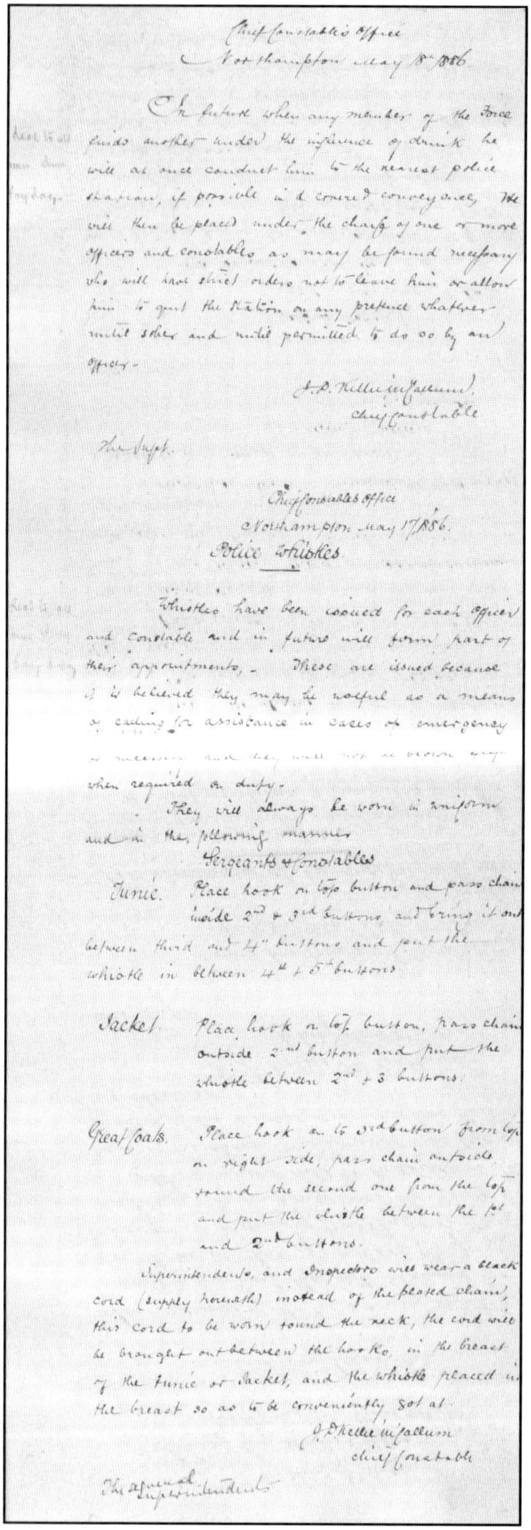

Chief Constable's Office
Northampton May 18th 1886

In future when any member of the Force finds another under the influence of drink he will at once conduct him to the nearest police station, if possible in a covered conveyance. He will then be placed under the charge of one or more officers and constables as may be found necessary who will have strict orders not to leave him or allow him to quit the station on any pretext whatever until sober and until permitted to do so by an officer.

J. D. Kellie MacCallum
Chief Constable

The Supt.

Chief Constables Office
Northampton May 17 1886.

Police Whistles

Whistles have been issued for each officer and constable and in future will form part of their appointments. These are issued because it is believed they may be useful as a means of calling for assistance in cases of emergency or necessity and they will not be blown except when required on duty.

They will always be worn in uniform and in the following manner

Sergeants & Constables

Tunic. Place hook on top button and pass chain inside 2nd & 3rd buttons and bring it out between third and 4th buttons and put the whistle in between 4th & 5th buttons

Jacket. Place hook on top button, pass chain outside 2nd button and put the whistle between 2nd & 3 buttons.

Great Coats. Place hook on to 3rd button from top on right side, pass chain outside round the second one from the top and put the whistle between the 1st and 2nd buttons.

Superintendents and Inspectors will wear a black cord (supply herewith) instead of the plated chain; this cord to be worn round the neck, the cord will be brought out between the hooks, in the breast of the tunic or jacket, and the whistle placed in the breast so as to be conveniently got at.

J. D. Kellie MacCallum
Chief Constable

The several Superintendents

Above: James Dalgleish Kellie-MacCallum, Chief Constable between 1881 and 1931. Even with fifty years' service, Kellie-MacCallum does not even get into the top ten of long serving Chief Constables. Born in Perthshire into Scottish landed gentry, following army service, Kellie-MacCallum was elected to be the Chief Constable of Northamptonshire in 1881, at the age of 36. Although not the longest serving Chief Constable, he was certainly the oldest when he retired in 1931 at the age of 86. Not surprisingly, he only lived a few months more, dying in September 1932 at Quinton near Northampton, where he is buried. *(Northamptonshire Police Museum)*

Left: Communication between the Chief Constable's office and the various Divisional Headquarters was by means of the Message Book. Messages from the Chief Constable would be written down in the book, and then the whole book sent on to the station concerned. The answer back would be a separate report. By this means, all the Chief Constable's messages would be contained in one easily referenced place. This is the Kettering Divisional Message Book, showing a memo of 17 May 1886 giving instructions on how to wear the newly issued whistles. *(Northamptonshire Police Museum)*

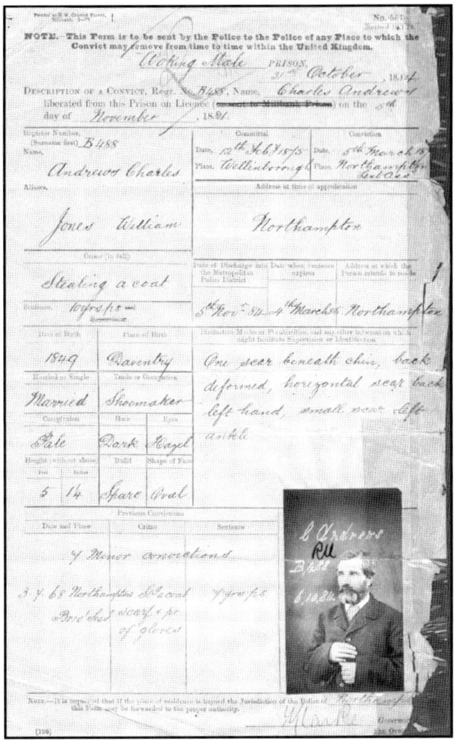

NOTE.—This Form is to be sent by the Police to the Police of any Place to which the Convict may remove from time to time within the United Kingdom.

Woking Male PRISON,
31st October, 1884

DESCRIPTION OF A CONVICT, Regr. No. B488, Name, Charles Andrews liberated from this Prison on Licence (~~or sent to Millbank Prison~~) on the 5th day of November, 1884.

Register Number, (Surname first) B488
Name, Andrews Charles
Aliases, Jones William

Committal: Date, 12th Feby 1875; Place, Wellingborough
Conviction: Date, 5th March 18[illegible]; Place, Northampton Genl Ass
Address at time of apprehension: Northampton

Crime (in full): Stealing a coat
Sentence: 10 yrs p.s.

Date of Discharge into the Metropolitan Police District: 5th Nov 84
Date when Sentence expires: 4th March 85
Address at which the Person intends to reside: Northampton

Date of Birth	Place of Birth
1849	Daventry

Married or Single	Trade or Occupation
Married	Shoemaker

Complexion	Hair	Eyes
Pale	Dark	Hazel

Height (without shoes) Feet	Inches	Build	Shape of Face
5	1¼	Spare	Oval

Distinctive Marks or Peculiarities, and any other information which might facilitate Supervision or Identification: One scar beneath chin, back deformed, horizontal scar back left hand, small scar left ankle

Previous Convictions

Date and Place	Crime	Sentence
4 Minor convictions		
3.7.68 Northampton Boro' Sess	Stg a coat scarf & pr of gloves	7 yrs p.s.

NOTE.—It is requested that if the place of residence is beyond the Jurisdiction of the Police of Northampton this Form may be forwarded to the proper authority.

(196)

Memo from Woking Prison, dated 31 October 1884, giving notification to a local police force that a convict is being released and is coming to live locally. After release, convicts were required to report to the local police at regular intervals. Charles Andrews, who has just served ten years' penal servitude for the theft of one coat, was coming to live in Duston, then in the county, and this notification, plus photograph, was sent to the Northamptonshire County Constabulary to make sure he reported to them. *(Northamptonshire Police Museum)*

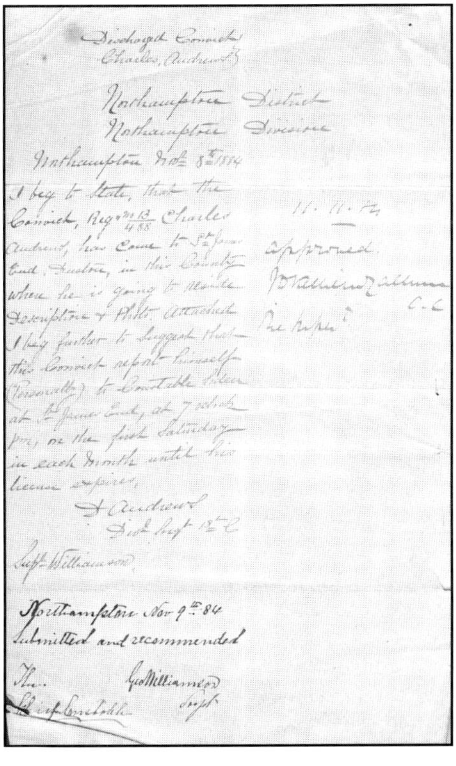

Discharged Convict
Charles Andrews

Northampton District
Northampton Division
Northampton Nov 8th 1884

I beg to state, that the Convict, Regr No B 488 Charles Andrews, has come to St James End, Duston, in this County where he is going to reside. Description & Photo attached. I beg further to suggest that this Convict report himself (Personally) to Constable [illegible] at St James End, at 7 o'clock pm, on the first Saturday in each month until his licence expires.

L Andrews
Dist Sergt 1st C

Supt Williamson

11.11.84
Approved
[illegible]
C.C.

Northampton Nov 9th 84
Submitted and recommended
The Chief Constable
Geo Williamson
Supt

The report made by Sergeant Levi Andrews (presumably no relation), suggesting that Charles Andrews reports himself at 7 p.m. on the first Saturday in every month until his licence (a type of parole) runs out. This went to the Chief Constable for approval. *(Northamptonshire Police Museum)*

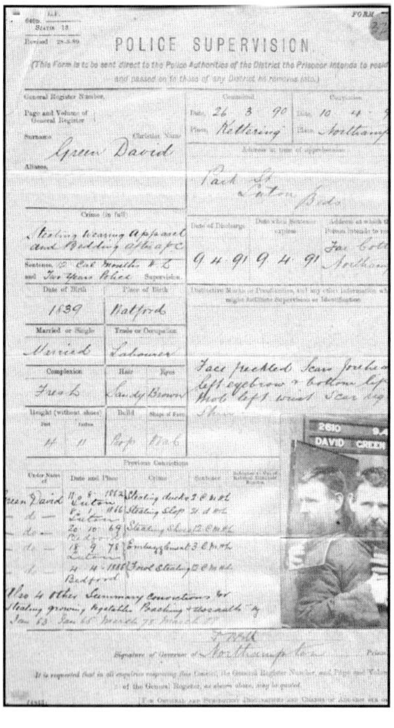

POLICE SUPERVISION

(This Form is to be sent direct to the Police Authorities of the District the Prisoner intends to reside and passed on to those of any District he removes into.)

Surname: Green Christian Name: David

Committed: Date 26 3 90 Place Kettering

Address at time of apprehension: Park St Luton Beds

Crime (in full): Stealing wearing apparel and Bedding ...

Date of Birth: 1839 Place of Birth: Watford

Married or Single: Married Trade or Occupation: Labourer

Complexion: Fresh Hair: Sandy Brown

Above: Wellingborough town strength, 1890s. Sitting on the extreme left is Superintendent John Alexander, of the 1892 case of Penn *v* Alexander. William Penn, a local landlord was, according to the police, illegally opening on Sunday by serving 'locals' instead of the 'bona fide travellers' he was only entitled to. Penn was convicted, but consistently appealed, eventually to the House of Lords, but always had his conviction upheld. With today's lax drinking laws, this is difficult to understand, but until the licensing laws were changed during the First World War, Penn *v* Alexander was the stated case for Sunday opening of public houses. *(Author's Collection)*

Left: A Police Supervision notice, issued to the police of the locality when a convict was to be released from prison. In this case, David Green was being released from Northampton Gaol, and was going to live in Far Cotton, which, until 1900, was in the jurisdiction of the County Constabulary. It is to be wondered why David Green, with a string of convictions, only got twelve months for theft of clothes, while Charles Andrews (see upper photograph on page 73) got ten years for the theft of a coat. *(Northamptonshire Police Museum)*

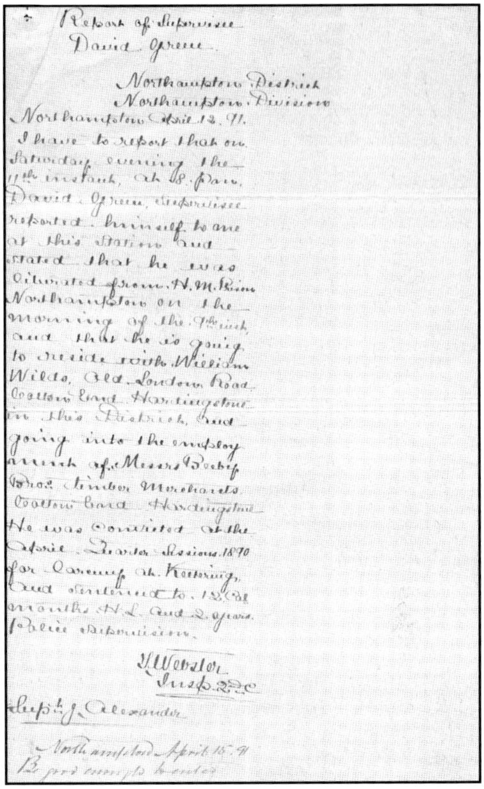
Report of Supervisee
David Green

Northampton District
Northampton Division

Northampton April 13. 91.

I have to report that on Saturday evening the 11th instant, at 8 p.m. David Green, supervisee reported himself to me at this Station and stated that he was liberated from H.M. Prison Northampton on the morning of the 9th inst, and that he is going to reside with William Wilds, Old London Road Cotton End Hardingstone in this District, and going into the employment of Messrs Beeby Bros. timber Merchants Cotton End Hardingstone. He was convicted at the April Quarter Sessions 1890 for Larceny at Kettering, and sentenced to 12 Cal months H.L. and 2 years Police Supervision.

T. Webster
Insp. 2 C

Supt. J. Alexander

Northampton April 15. 91
Be good enough to enter

The report from Thomas Webster, Inspector of the Northampton Division of the County Constabulary, concerning David Green. The report went all the way up the chain of command to the Chief Constable, who alone made the final decision. *(Northamptonshire Police Museum)*

PC136, Albert Clarke, in 1899. This photograph illustrates the uniform worn at the turn of the nineteenth into the twentieth century. Two types of head-dress were worn – the helmet and the patrol cap. This picture shows the helmet, which is like the modern one but is much decorated with a spike and a large badge, and was only worn during the summer months or on special occasions, such as the Quarter Sessions or the Assizes. The double-peaked patrol cap (see top of page 71) was worn during the winter months, and either a lighter single-peaked patrol cap or the helmet was worn during the summer. *(Northamptonshire Police Museum)*

Hector Daniel Macleod, the first police officer in the world to arrest a fleeing criminal after a car chase. In April 1899, Frederick Phillips, posing as an advance publicity man for Barnum and Bailey's circus, conned money out of lady shopkeepers in the suburbs of Northampton. After a complaint from one Jane Botterill, and finding out that the miscreant was fleeing town, Sergeant Macleod commandeered a Benz motorcar belonging to Jack Harrison who lived in Marefair, and with Harrison at the wheel, gave chase. Phillips was caught between Harpole and Flore and brought back to Northampton. *(Northamptonshire Police Museum)*

Angel Lane police station, 1900. Needing more space in Northampton, a new police station was built in Angel Lane, at the back of the headquarters in George Row. The building is now used by local government. The building on the extreme right was once the old County Gaol, and the large notice on the centre gate is on the site of the 'New Drop' permanent gallows. Eighteen men and two women were publicly hanged on this spot between 1819 and 1852. *(Author's Collection)*

By 1900, the town of Rushden had rapidly expanded due to the shoe-making boom and needed a larger police station. Rushden police station was built in 1900, and lasted seventy-five years before being demolished in 1975, to be replaced by today's charmless building. Before its demise, the television series *Hunter's Walk* used Rushden police station as a stage set, so it had the distinction of being the best-known police station in Britain for a number of years. *(Northamptonshire Police Museum)*

The Wellingborough town strength showing off their new uniforms in 1904. The patrol caps were still being worn, but this new style of tunic had five buttons and two breast pockets. The constable sitting on a chair on the far left is wearing the single stripe and collar star of the Merit Class. On first joining, men were Third Class Constables, with advancement to Second Class and First Class, depending on competence. The Merit Class was higher than the First Class, and only given to constables of exceptional prowess. Promotion to Sergeant only came from the First Class or Merit Class. *(Northamptonshire Police Museum)*

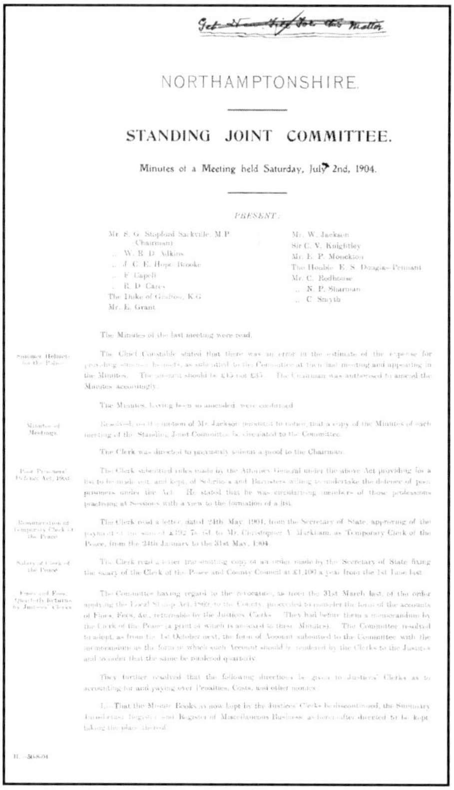

NORTHAMPTONSHIRE.

STANDING JOINT COMMITTEE.

Minutes of a Meeting held Saturday, July 2nd, 1904.

PRESENT:

Mr. S. G. Stopford Sackville, M.P. (Chairman)	Mr. W. Jackson
" W. B. D. Adkins	Sir C. V. Knightley
" J. C. E. Hope-Brooke	Mr. E. P. Monckton
" F. Capell	The Honble. E. S. Douglas-Pennant
" R. D. Carey	Mr. C. Rodhouse
The Duke of Grafton, K.G.	" N. P. Sharman
Mr. E. Grant	" C. Smyth

The Minutes of the last meeting were read.

Summer Helmets for the Police. The Chief Constable stated that there was an error in the estimate of the expense for providing summer helmets, as submitted to the Committee at their last meeting and appearing in the Minutes. The amount should be £15 not £35. The Chairman was authorised to amend the Minutes accordingly.

The Minutes, having been so amended, were confirmed.

Minutes of Meetings. Resolved, on the motion of Mr. Jackson pursuant to notice, that a copy of the Minutes of each meeting of the Standing Joint Committee be circulated to the Committee.

The Clerk was directed to previously submit a proof to the Chairman.

Poor Prisoners' Defence Act, 1903. The Clerk submitted rules made by the Attorney General under the above Act providing for a list to be made out, and kept, of Solicitors and Barristers willing to undertake the defence of poor prisoners under the Act. He stated that he was circularising members of those professions practising at Sessions with a view to the formation of a list.

Remuneration of Temporary Clerk of the Peace. The Clerk read a letter, dated 24th May, 1904, from the Secretary of State, approving of the payment of the sum of £192 7s. 6d. to Mr. Christopher A. Markham, as Temporary Clerk of the Peace, from the 24th January to the 31st May, 1904.

Salary of Clerk of the Peace. The Clerk read a letter transmitting copy of an order made by the Secretary of State fixing the salary of the Clerk of the Peace and County Council at £1,100 a year from the 1st June last.

Fines and Fees. Quarterly Returns by Justices' Clerks. The Committee having regard to the revocation, as from the 31st March last, of the order applying the Local Stamp Act, 1869, to the County, proceeded to consider the form of the accounts of Fines, Fees, &c., returnable by the Justices' Clerks. They had before them a memorandum by the Clerk of the Peace (a print of which is annexed to these Minutes). The Committee resolved to adopt, as from the 1st October next, the form of Account submitted to the Committee with the memorandum as the form in which such Account should be rendered by the Clerks to the Justices and to order that the same be rendered quarterly.

They further resolved that the following directions be given to Justices' Clerks as to accounting for and paying over Penalties, Costs, and other monies:

1.—That the Minute Books as now kept by the Justices' Clerks be discontinued, the Summary Jurisdiction Register and Register of Miscellaneous Business, as hereinafter directed to be kept, taking the place thereof.

H. [illegible]

Left: After the Local Government Act of 1888, the police authority in the counties became the Standing Joint Committee, so named because it consisted of Magistrates and elected County Councillors. The Standing Joint Committee in a county did not have quite the same powers as a Watch Committee in a borough. This is the first page of the published Minutes to the Standing Joint Committee of 15 October 1904. The Committee still meets, but is now called the Police Authority, and has a different ratio of Magistrates to County Councillors. *(Northamptonshire Police Museum)*

Below: Out of hours activities, especially sport, was encouraged in the County Constabulary. This is Kettering Police Football Club in 1904. Standing in the back row on the extreme right is Sergeant Esau Dunn, who eventually became the Superintendent at Towcester. His grandson, Richard Dunn, also became a Superintendent at Kettering in the 1980s. The majority of officers in this photograph reached their pensions, although PC Saint, with the ball, was dismissed two months after this photograph was taken for being absent from duty and refusing to say where he had been! *(Northamptonshire Police Museum)*

This car crash near Towcester on 3 February 1907 was still such a novelty as to attract quite a crowd. Thankfully, no one was killed. Emma Mills became the county's first fatal casualty of a motorcar accident eight years later when she was killed at Wootton at 11 p.m. on Saturday 5 June 1915. The driver of the car, Thomas Taffinder, was found not guilty of manslaughter. *(Northamptonshire Police Museum)*

By the time this photograph was taken, during the great military exercise in Northamptonshire in 1913, the patrol cap had been abandoned, and the helmet, with the same size badge as the patrol cap, was worn all year round. The constable on the right is PC Lattimer, who, when he was recalled to the army during the First World War, won the Distinguished Conduct Medal during the capture of Jerusalem by General Allenby in December 1917. His daughter, Margaret, was secretary to four Chief Constables (Bolton, Gott, Cutting and Buck) before retiring after fifty years' service. *(Northamptonshire Police Museum)*

Left: PC Benjamin Street. A Staffordshire man, born in Bilston, Benjamin Street joined the Northamptonshire County Constabulary in March 1908 following army service. As a member of the Army Reserve, he was recalled to the colours on 2 August 1914, joining the 4th Battalion, the Grenadier Guards. On 28 September 1915, Street died of wounds received in action. He is buried in the Lillers Communal cemetery, near Bethune in France. *(Northamptonshire Police Museum)*

Below: War Memorial tablets in Wootton Hall. Eleven County Constabulary police officers died in the First World War (H. Ayres, P. Benjamin, W. Billing, W. Callow, A. Knight, J. Warwick, S. Lane, W. Packer, W. Shaw, A. Smith, B. Street); and three in the Second World War (H. Baker, F. Griffiths, F. Walden). The Borough Police lost two officers in the First World War (J. Adnitt, H. Bignell); and two in the Second World War (T. Brady, F. Elms). *(Author's Collection)*

Right: The fear of sabotage was very real during the First World War; this is the Harringworth Viaduct being guarded. The Sergeant is George Brumby. *(Northamptonshire Police Museum)*

Below: As with the Northampton Borough, the Special Constabulary was a source of manpower for the County Constabulary as well. These are the Special Constables of Kettering during the First World War. As these men were obviously only serving for the duration, expensive uniforms were foregone. *(Northamptonshire Police Museum)*

The Kettering Special Constabulary Mobile Section, again with no uniforms. *(Northamptonshire Police Museum)*

The Kettering town strength, 1922. The Superintendent is Henry Tebbey, who came to Kettering as a Superintendent after the death of William Hooper in April 1922; the Inspector is Edward Jones, who was promoted in October 1921. The Sergeant sitting third from left in the front row is Sergeant Lionel Swan, wearing the ribbon of the Military Medal awarded during the First World War. The constable standing on the extreme left in the second row is PC Ian Brian Pratt. Apparently he used to answer the telephone by saying 'I.B. Pratt. Who be you?' You could get away with things like that in those days. *(Author's Collection)*

The Wellingborough town strength, 1920s. Sitting in the centre is Superintendent Macleod (see photograph at the top of page 76). Sergeant Harry Roughton, sitting third from the left in the front row, was awarded the Distinguished Conduct Medal and Military Cross during the First World War. While working as a reporter, the famous novelist H.E. Bates, in his autobiography, gave his opinion 'that on the whole the police of Wellingborough at that time, on or off duty, were the most uncouth, most bog-headed, most foul-mouthed collection of humans I had ever met'. Because the dates coincide, Bates would have been referring to some of the police officers in this photograph! *(Northamptonshire Police Museum)*

As with the Borough Police, the County Constabulary had to send men away to police the General Strike of 1926. In fact, two squads were sent away: one went to Bentinck Colliery and the other went with their Borough colleagues to the Hucknall Colliery, both being in Nottinghamshire. This is the 'official' photograph of the Bentinck Colliery squad. The officer sitting on the extreme left is a constable of the Nottinghamshire County Constabulary, attached to the squad as a local guide. *(Northamptonshire Police Museum)*

And this is the 'unofficial' photograph. Who says that policemen don't have a sense of humour? *(Northamptonshire Police Museum)*

The Hucknall Colliery squad, with the owner and manager seated in the centre. The constable riding the motorcycle is the local guide. Sitting on the extreme right is PC William Baird, who, along with medal ribbons of the Boer War and Great War, also wears the ribbon of the Belgian *Croix de Guerre*, awarded in September 1919. Sitting on the left is PC Charles Bates, wearing the ribbon of the King's Police Medal. In 1926, PC Bates was the first police officer of constable rank to be awarded the King's Police Medal for Meritorious Service, as opposed to a gallantry award. *(Author's Collection)*

Like the Borough Police, after the great Road Traffic Act of 1930, the County Constabulary established dedicated road traffic divisions. This is the traffic division stationed at Kettering in the mid-1930s, which was presumably responsible for the whole of the north of the county. *(Northamptonshire Police Museum)*

This car was stationed at Weedon for the Towcester Division. PC Frank Whitlock is on the right, with PC Syd Richardson. The make of the car is unknown, although it is probably an Alvis. *(Author's Collection)*

The Wellingborough Division strength of 1936. This is the retirement photograph of Superintendent Edward Jones (seated in the centre of the front row, wearing the Sam Browne belt), who was promoted from Kettering to Wellingborough in May 1928. He is also wearing the ribbon of the Silver Jubilee medal of 1935, which was traditionally given to all men who had been in the force at the time of that particular monarch's Coronation (on this occasion, 1910). Sitting third from the left in the front row is Sergeant Ernest Farram, who would be awarded the Royal Humane Society Silver Medal for his actions at the Irchester Tannery Disaster of August 1938. In the space of four minutes, five men had been overcome by poisonous fumes while clearing an effluent tank. Donning breathing apparatus, Sergeant Farram descended into the pit to tie ropes round the men. Unfortunately, all five had already died. Despite the breathing apparatus, Sergeant Farram was affected by the fumes, and had to hitchhike to hospital as there was no vehicle available to transport him. *(Northamptonshire Police Museum)*

When James Kellie-MacCallum retired as Chief Constable after fifty years with the force, Angus Arthur Ferguson became the new Chief Constable. The son of Sir Arthur Ferguson, the Scottish Inspector of Constabulary, Angus Ferguson had been commissioned into the army after leaving Cambridge University, before joining the Edinburgh City Police. In June 1931, at the age of 27 years and 10 months, he was appointed Chief Constable of Northamptonshire. Because of his unswerving application of the Discipline Code, he was never very popular. He resigned in 1941 to return to the army. *(Northamptonshire Police Museum)*

Police recruitment stopped during the Second World War. The police strength was then augmented from three sources: the Special Constabulary, the First Police Reserve (recently retired policemen called back) and the Police War Reserve (untrained men who contracted to serve as policemen for the duration). This is the Special Constabulary for E Section; the Kettering district. From left to right, back row: T.J. Bosworth, W.H. Cawkill, H.C.C. Richardson, J.F. Longstaff, A.C. Waller, L.W. Collyer, T.B.J. Wilby. Front row: H.M. Kirby, Inspector E.J. Seddon, Commandant E.C. Gravestock, Superintendent A.J. Chapman, Inspector A.W. Gravestock, R.G. Almond, G.R. Bult. Superintendent Arthur Chapman, of the regular constabulary, was in charge of Kettering and Corby. *(Northamptonshire Police Museum)*

And nearly the same officers in uniform, at the back of Kettering police station. *(Northamptonshire Police Museum)*

What is believed to be the combined Special Constabulary of Kettering and Corby, together with some of their regular colleagues in helmets, *c.* 1939. This was taken at Corby police station, which, at that time, was at the West Gate of the Steel Works, near the railway bridge on Rockingham Road. Why the man on the extreme left and the man second from the right are wearing armlets is unknown – the County Constabulary never wore armlets. *(Northamptonshire Police Museum)*

Special Constables stationed at Higham Ferrers, 1940. Angus Ferguson, the Chief Constable, is seated in the middle of the front row. He resigned a few months after this photograph was taken to return to the army. On the extreme right in the back row is Eric Quincey, who joined the Specials during the General Strike of 1926. Eventually becoming the County Commandant, he retired in 1981 after fifty-five years' service. *(Author's Collection)*

Robert Henry Dundas Bolton took over as Chief Constable from Angus Ferguson in 1941. Originally in the army, seeing service in India, 'Bertie' eventually joined the Metropolitan Police under the Trenchard System (direct officer entry, where public school/university-educated boys joined the police as Inspectors). 'Bertie' Bolton retired in 1960 and returned to live in London. He is seen here presenting a Police Long Service Medal. *(Northamptonshire Police Museum)*

'Bertie' always insisted on being called 'Captain' Bolton. One story has it that a PC, being welcomed back to the force in 1946 after army service, on being ushered into the Chief's office, was greeted by 'Bertie' with a brusque: 'I'm Captain Bolton', to which the PC replied, 'Well in that case, I'm Major —' which had been his wartime rank. A Major outranks a Captain, so it should have been the Chief Constable standing for the PC, and not vice-versa. After that, perhaps it is not surprising that the PC never got promoted. *(Northamptonshire Police Museum)*

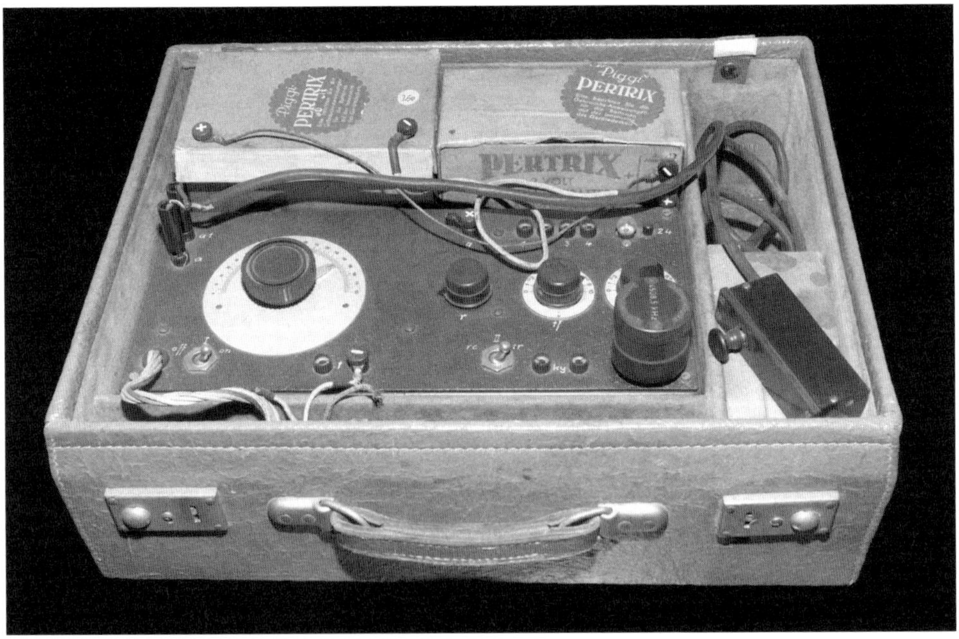

The British MI5 were puzzled by German incompetence in the early part of the Second World War. During three months in 1940, twenty-one German agents (some unable to speak English) parachuted into England and were all captured within hours. One of them, Swedish born Gösta Caroli, landed near Denton with this transmitter strapped to his chest. The extra weight dragged him forward as he landed, and he was knocked unconscious. Caroli was later to become a double agent (code-named 'Summer'). This transmitter, one of the few to survive, is now preserved in the Police Museum. *(Northamptonshire Police Museum)*

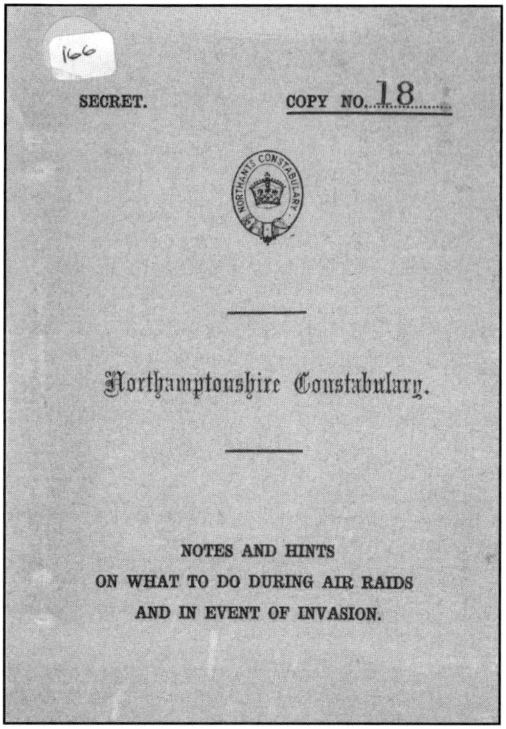
166

SECRET. COPY NO. 18

NORTHANTS CONSTABULARY

Northamptonshire Constabulary.

NOTES AND HINTS
ON WHAT TO DO DURING AIR RAIDS
AND IN EVENT OF INVASION.

A handbook issued to every member of the force in February 1942. *(Northamptonshire Police Museum)*

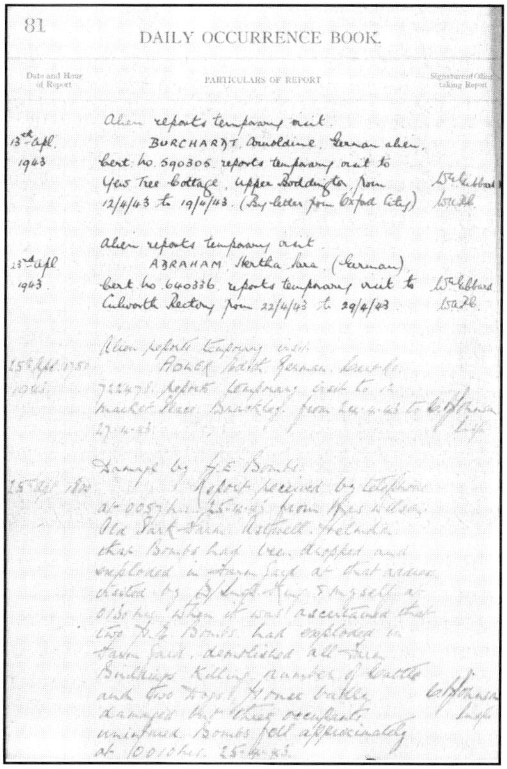
81

DAILY OCCURRENCE BOOK.

Date and Hour of Report	PARTICULARS OF REPORT	Signature of Officer taking Report
13th Apl. 1943	Alien reports temporary visit. BURCHARDT, Arnoldine, German alien. Cert. No. 590305 reports temporary visit to Yew Tree Cottage, Upper Boddington, from 12/4/43 to 19/4/43. (By letter from Oxford City)	
23rd Apl 1943	Alien reports temporary visit. ABRAHAM, Hertha Sara (German). Cert. No. 640336 reports temporary visit to Culworth Rectory from 22/4/43 to 29/4/43	
25th Apl 1943	Alien reports temporary visit.	
25th Apl	Damage by H.E. Bombs. Report received by telephone	

Occurrence Books were kept at large stations, instead of individual diaries of the one-man beats. These recorded every incident, and provided a valuable 'running log', which would immediately put you 'in the picture' when returning after a few days' absence. Regrettably, these are no longer kept, and future historians will not have such a valuable source to consult – as we can now do. This is page 81 from the Brackley Occurrence Book, 1934–1948, recording enemy bombs falling at Helmdon on the night of 25 April 1943. Also note the visits that 'aliens' had to make. *(Northamptonshire Police Museum)*

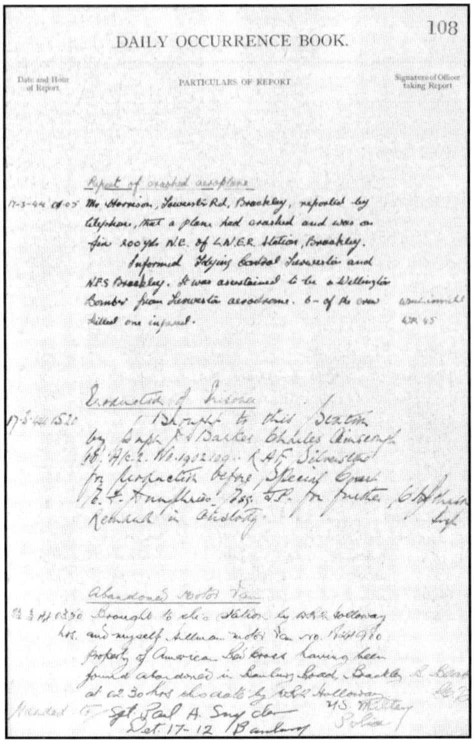

108

DAILY OCCURRENCE BOOK.

Date and Hour of Report	PARTICULARS OF REPORT	Signature of Officer taking Report
	Report of crashed aeroplane	
17-3-44 01.05	Mr Harrison, Towcester Rd, Brackley, reported by telephone, that a plane had crashed and was on fire 200 yds N.E. of L.N.E.R. Station, Brackley. Informed Flying Control Silverstone and N.F.S. Brackley. It was ascertained to be a Wellington Bomber from Silverstone aerodrome. 6 of the crew killed one injured.	W.M. Linnell WR 45
	[illegible]	
17-3-44 1520	[illegible] brought to this Station by [illegible] R.A.F. Silverstone for [illegible] before Special [illegible] [illegible] [illegible] in Custody.	[illegible]
	Abandoned Motor Van	
18-3-44 0230 hrs.	Brought to this station by W.R.C. Holloway and myself Hillman motor van no. [illegible] property of American Red Cross having been found abandoned in Banbury Road, Brackley at 02.30 hrs this date by W.R.C. Holloway. Handed to Sgt. Paul A. Snyder U.S. Military Police Det. 17-12 Banbury	[illegible]

Left: Page 108 of the Brackley Occurrence Book, recording the crash of a Wellington bomber from RAF Silverstone on the night of 17 March 1944, with the loss of six crewmembers. The report is signed by W.M. Linnell W[ar] R[eserve] 45. *(Northamptonshire Police Museum)*

Below: As with the Borough Police on page 44, the County Constabulary was also inspected by Sir Llewellyn Atcherley in 1945. This is the inspection at Kettering, with 'Bertie' Bolton, the Chief Constable, and Superintendent Arthur Chapman, standing behind Sir Llewellyn. The PC on the extreme right is believed to be PC James Webb, who won the Military Medal during the First World War. Having just retired in 1939, he was brought back as a Police War Reserve. *(Northamptonshire Police Museum)*

Above: Eventually the war was over, and victory celebrations were held. This one was held at Kettering parish church and mainly consisted of the Special Constabulary. *(Northamptonshire Police Museum)*

Right: WPC Stella Parsons, the first Woman Police Constable of the Northamptonshire County Constabulary. Women had been employed by the County Constabulary during the Second World War as secretaries and drivers in the Women's Auxiliary Police Corps (WAPC) – but they were not trained police officers. WPC Parsons was sworn in on 1 September 1946. She had been in the WAPC, and later as a secretary at Angel Lane. A few weeks later, Miss Margaret Taylor and Miss Katherine Day were also enrolled. In 1948, Miss Parsons resigned upon her marriage. She currently enjoys retirement in Wellingborough. *(Northamptonshire Police Museum)*

The Wellingborough Divisional strength, 1946. The Superintendent (seated in the middle of the front row, with collar and tie) is William Roche, who was promoted and stationed at Wellingborough in April 1946. He remained there for the rest of his service, eventually retiring in 1967 after forty-four years' service. Roche Way in Wellingborough is named in his honour. Second from the left in the back row, wearing the flat cap, is a constable of the War Reserve, who would be 'stood down' in 1946. *(Northamptonshire Police Museum)*

Northamptonshire Constabulary Football XI, 1949/50 season. Sergeant Geoff Evans, seated second from the left, won the Military Medal during the Second World War. Superintendent Albert Norris (in uniform) had just been awarded the King's Police Medal for Meritorious Service in the New Year's Honours of 1949, and retired in 1957 after forty-three years' service. *(Northamptonshire Police Museum)*

The purchase of Wootton Hall and the 50-acre grounds in 1947 for £22,500 was one of the most astute moves ever made by the Police Authority. The original hall was demolished in 1911 due to dry rot, and the present hall built near to the spot. The building was, incidentally, rented by James Kellie-MacCallum on his arrival in the county, prior to his moving to Quinton. The photograph of him (see top of page 72) is quite clearly taken in front of one of the bow windows. *(Northamptonshire Police Museum)*

The original gateway to Wootton Hall. This has long gone, although one of the stone balls can be seen in the Police Museum. *(Northamptonshire Police Museum)*

The motorcycle section outside Wootton Hall in the mid-1950s. *(Northamptonshire Police Museum)*

The front of Wootton Hall, just after the extension on the right-hand side had been completed, in the mid-1970s. Today, this view is altered because a large gatehouse has been built in the foreground of this photograph. *(Northamptonshire Police Museum)*

An aerial view of Wootton Hall in 1947, when first purchased for the County Constabulary. This photograph shows the rear of the building. *(Northamptonshire Police Museum)*

An aerial view of Wootton Hall in the early 1990s. This photograph shows the front of the building, with extensions. In 2007, the wing in the top right was demolished and rebuilt to provide more office space. *(Northamptonshire Police Museum)*

By 1951, the regular police service still had no long service medal, although the Special Constabulary had had a long service medal since 1918. So in June 1951, the Police Long Service Medal was established, for twenty-two years' approved service, and was awarded to all serving officers having the required length of service. It was not made retroactive. This is the parade at Wootton Hall when the first Police Long Service Medals were issued. *(Northamptonshire Police Museum)*

Because the force had room to breathe at Wootton Hall, instead of cramped up in George Row, modern technology could be used, and that meant, of course, radio. A modern control room was established, and the Home Office provided the expertise for seven patrol cars to be equipped with two-way radio. So, in February 1951, Northamptonshire became one of the first county forces to have radio. This came into its own when the London to Liverpool Express crashed at Stowe Tunnel, near Weedon, on 21 September 1951. *(Northamptonshire Police Museum)*

Eight people were killed and forty-two injured. Because of radio communications with the patrol cars sent to the scene, rescue operations could be coordinated with more purpose than they had been previously. As a result, all fifty casualties were evacuated from the scene within an incredible sixty-three minutes after the crash. *(Northamptonshire Police Museum)*

Because of the growth of Corby after the Second World War, the old police station near the West Gate of the British Steel Works on Rockingham Road became inadequate. This photograph was taken in the late 1940s or early '50s, just before the move to the new police station in Elizabeth Street. This building later reverted to use by the British Steel Corporation, but has now been demolished. *(Northamptonshire Police Museum)*

The new Corby police station was opened by the Home Secretary, Gwilym Lloyd-George, in June 1956. This photograph was taken just before the opening, and shows the building being finished. Three years later, the Magistrates' Court building was added to the left side. The fields in the distance to the right would soon be built over by the Exeter estate. *(Northamptonshire Police Museum)*

An inspection of Police Cadets by Sergeant Spiller and PC Humphries at Wootton Hall, 1969. The cadet system was started by 'Bertie' Bolton in 1954 as a recruiting device, when conventional recruiting was at a low ebb. Young men, and eventually young women, served as cadets straight from school, until they joined the regular service at the age of 19. The Northamptonshire Police Cadets lasted until January 1982, when the system was abolished. *(Northamptonshire Police Museum)*

Northamptonshire Police Cadets marching in front of Wootton Hall in the late 1970s – note the ladies' new style hats. There was an argument 'for' and 'against' the cadet system. As a recruiting device, it was second to none; but joining straight from school, and then entering full-time police work, meant that no other perspective on life except the police point of view could be gained. But be that as it may, the cadet system in this county has now been extinct for twenty-five years, and is unlikely to return. *(Northamptonshire Police Museum)*

Officers from the Kettering Division – winners of the Chief Constable's Ambulance Cup in 1956. Superintendent Arthur Chapman is in plain clothes. Standing in the back row on the extreme right is PC Peter Holyoak. *(Northamptonshire Police Museum)*

On 1 April 1956, the EOKA rebellion started on Cyprus, which aimed to reunite Cyprus with Greece in the movement called Enosis. Because of infiltration by EOKA, it was felt that the Cyprus Police could not provide a trustworthy policing presence, and thus a United Kingdom Police Unit (UKU) was sent to Cyprus. Between 1956 and 1960 when Cyprus gained independence, 895 British police officers were attached for various periods to the UKU. Being armed at all times, the UKU members received this pamphlet emphasizing the very real dangers. Six British police officers were murdered by EOKA. *(P. Holyoak)*

RESTRICTED

READ AND KEEP THIS IT–MAY SAVE YOUR LIFE

Men have been killed and wounded lately through their own carelessness. Every Policeman and Government Official is an E.O.K.A. target.

The following instructions are a guide to help you in your normal day to day routine duties. They do not cover all aspects of precautions that can be taken but if remembered will stand you in good stead and may well deter an assailant.

Always remember that a potential assailant can study you without your knowing it and always has that advantage. You must be on the watch at all times. Remember above all that HABIT may destroy.

1. A. Always carry a loaded revolver.
   B. DON'T, unless quite unavoidable, go out alone unarmed.
2. A. If it is necessary to shoot in self-protection or in protection of another, **stand steady**, shoot quickly and accurately.
   B. DON'T attempt to shoot at an assailant whilst **you** are running, you will not hit him.
3. A. If **you** have a driver bodyguard, use him at all times on or off duty.
   B. DON'T just take a chance and not take your bodyguard with you.
4. A. Keep **changing** your routes and times to and from places you are visiting.
   B. DON'T use the **same** route every day at the **same** time.
5. A. Keep your eyes open for persons lurking in the vicinity of your house, office or Police Station when you enter or leave.
   B. DON'T walk out of your house, office or Police Station dreaming and not knowing what goes on about you.
6. A. Be constantly alert whenever youths on bicycles are in your vicinity.
   B. DON'T ignore youths on bicycles.
7. A. When driving your car place your revolver under your right thigh, so as to be in easy reach of your hand.
   B. DON'T have your pistol where you cannot get at it whilst driving your car yourself.

(2)

8. A. Have your revolver in your hand whilst travelling as a passenger in a vehicle.
   B. DON'T have your pistol where you cannot get at it whilst riding as a passenger in a vehicle.
9. A. Avoid as much as possible routes that may lead you into **traffic jams.**
   B. DON'T use **routes** that are prone to traffic jams.
10. A. **Keep moving.** Far better to back out and change direction than be stuck in some narrow street.
    B. DON'T stop your vehicle and just sit waiting to move, and not keep an eye on what goes on about you.
11. A. When in your quarters check your telephone from time to time to ascertain that it is in working order.
    B. DON'T just ignore your telephone and expect it to work when you want it to.
12. A. Always let a male member of your household answer all calls at night.
    B. DON'T let a female member of your household answer it at night. The other side may think that no males are in the house and take advantage of it.
13. A. **Always** answer your door **armed** and be on the **alert.**
    B. DON'T just take a chance and answer the door unarmed, and think that the other side would not dare to come to your door.

(3)

Left: Both county forces supplied volunteers to the UKU. Northampton Borough sent PC R. Cockrum and PC C. Warner. Northamptonshire County sent PC J. Oakenson, PC R. Russell, PC T. Pell, PC R. Watson, PC P. Holyoak, PS R. Willey and WPC M. Keaveny. In Cyprus, officers moved up a rank and received a new number, so British Constables became Sergeants and so on. This is County PC143 Peter Holyoak (PS2870, UKU) in winter uniform in Ledra Street, Nicosia, nicknamed 'Murder Mile' because of the many shootings which occurred there. Every county UKU volunteer returned home unharmed. *(P. Holyoak)*

The M1 motorway was opened in November 1959, and it is ironic to think that Northamptonshire, the second smallest county force, should have had the greatest number of miles of motorway to patrol: 27.6 miles. Two Ford estate cars were fitted out specifically for motorway use. Each car covered 71,000 miles during the first year, which necessitated adding this car, a Humber Snipe estate in 1960, when this photograph was taken. Note the traffic (or lack of it) on the actual carriageway. *(Northamptonshire Police Museum)*

By the early 1960s, Angel Lane police station was far too cramped to be suitable for a modern police station. Thus, in 1963 Angel Lane was relinquished after sixty-three years, and the Northampton South Sub-Divisional Headquarters moved into a new purpose-built police station at Mere Way, which had been carved from a corner of Wootton Park. As it was much closer to the M1 motorway, it became the station for the M1 patrols. It was opened in September 1963 by Mr W. Willis, HM Inspector of Constabulary, and is now employed as administrative offices. *(Northamptonshire Police Museum)*

The Northamptonshire County Constabulary was also capable of winning the Marquess of Northampton Cup for First Aid (see also top of page 24). This is the winning team, in 1966; all officers were stationed in Kettering. The figure of PC Peter Moody, standing on right, was always unmistakable because of his magnificent 'handlebar' moustache. The cup is no longer competed for and is housed in St John County Headquarters in Northampton. The smaller cup is the Chief Constable's Ambulance Cup. Again, this is no longer competed for, and is housed in the Police Museum at Wootton Hall. *(Northamptonshire Police Museum)*

John Aidan Hastings Gott was appointed Chief Constable of the Northamptonshire County Constabulary in 1960, on 'Bertie' Bolton's retirement. After leaving Oxford University, he joined the Metropolitan Police in 1937 under the Trenchard System. His rescue of a man from a bomb-damaged building during the London Blitz earned him the George Medal. When police officers were allowed into the armed forces, John Gott was commissioned into the RAF. In April 1945, at RAF East Kirby, he was awarded the MBE for Gallantry for his rescue of the dead and injured from a burning trolley of exploding bombs. *(Northamptonshire Police Museum)*

4

Northampton & County Constabulary, 1966–1974

Returning to police service after the Second World War, John Gott joined the Hertfordshire County Constabulary, and was Chief Superintendent in 1960 when he was elected to become Chief Constable of Northamptonshire. It was Gott who supervised the amalgamation of the County Constabulary with the Borough Police in 1966 to form the Northampton and County Constabulary, becoming its first Chief Constable. *(Northamptonshire Police Museum)*

John Gott and his personal car, showing off some of the trophies he had won. Unfortunately, the names of the trophies, together with the Sergeant, are unknown. The Sergeant is wearing the medal ribbon of the Distinguished Flying Cross, so he could have been an old RAF colleague. Devoted to the motorcar, Gott sat on many Home Office committees concerned with traffic laws. On Sunday 3 September 1972, Gott was racing his car around the Lydden Circuit in Kent when he had a heart attack at the wheel. The car failed to negotiate a bend and Gott was killed instantly. *(Northamptonshire Police Museum)*

The funeral of John Gott at All Saints Church, Northampton, September 1972. The cortège is approaching along George Row with, appropriately enough, the old County Constabulary Headquarters in the background to the left. Chief Superintendent Thomas Nicholson is leading the cortège. *(Northamptonshire Police Museum)*

Pallbearers carry John Gott's coffin after the service. His Chief Constable's cap and medals are on top. The sudden death of John Gott caused an interregnum of four months, during which time the force was in the hands of the Deputy Chief Constable, Stanley Church. *(Northamptonshire Police Museum)*

Frederick Cutting was chosen to succeed John Gott in January 1973. A native of Brighton, Cutting had joined the Brighton County Borough Police in 1948. After a short period back in industry, he joined the Bournemouth County Borough Police in 1953. In 1965, as a Superintendent, he transferred to the East Sussex County Constabulary. A year later he was appointed Assistant Chief Constable of the Warwickshire County Constabulary, before coming to Northamptonshire in 1973. Frederick Cutting retired on medical grounds in 1980, and now lives in Dorset. *(Northamptonshire Police Museum)*

Frederick Cutting substantially increased spending on the force, with new equipment. Until then, the patrol cars were Wolseley 16/90 models, painted black. This one, seen leaving Wellingborough police station, is being driven by PC Tony Hickman. *(Author's Collection)*

The new patrol car was chosen as the BLMC 2200, this time painted white, with 'go-faster' stripes along the side, in complete contrast to the plain black of the Wolseleys. This one, seen here in March 1973, is escorting a wide load at the summit of Rockingham Hill, heading for Corby steel works. The passenger is PC David 'Chip' Joiner with the author at the wheel. *(Author's Collection)*

Above: Modern patrol cars needed modern garaging as well. This photograph, taken in 1972 at the garages at Wootton Hall, shows legendary 'Jock' Thin, the chief mechanic, demonstrating the wonders of the 2200 to a group of cadets. 'Jock' Thin was the only mechanic that John Gott trusted to maintain his racing car. *(Northamptonshire Police Museum)*

Right: The uniform eventually adopted after the amalgamation: a tunic with four buttons and two breast pockets, but no hip pockets and no belt. Note the addition of 'collar dogs' or collar badges which represent hides of leather – denoting the staple industry of the county – upon which is superimposed a Northamptonshire Rose. *(Northamptonshire Police Museum)*

Since 1954, an annual cup had been awarded to the 'Cadet of the Year'. This photograph shows Ian Hutchins receiving the trophy from Mr Stanley Peck, HM Inspector of Constabulary, on his annual inspection, in 1972 – the last year of the competition before the cadets were disbanded. PC160 Hutchins eventually became an Inspector. *(Northamptonshire Police Museum)*

The Northampton and County Constabulary Cadets football team, late 1960s. Standing, from left to right: P. Collyer, I. Peet, M. Shanahan, B. Law, D. Hill, P. Foode, J. Doherty. Front row: W. Shoebridge, P. Mundy, Chief Inspector V. Allen, PC E. Humphries (trainer), T. Kavanagh, P. Vickers. Later, as a Superintendent, Phil Vickers was awarded the MBE in the 1998 New Year's Honours list for the policing arrangements for the funeral of Diana, Princess of Wales at Althorp. *(M. Shanahan)*

5

Northamptonshire Police, 1974–Present

Mr Cutting oversaw the change of name to Northamptonshire Police in 1974, under the Local Government Act, plus the unsuitable boundary changes that went with it. When he retired in 1981, Maurice Buck (pictured) was appointed Chief Constable. He immediately set about a complete reorganisation of the force, including boundary changes. He also introduced the concept of 'Policing by Objectives' which, for whatever reasons, never proved popular. Mr Buck retired in 1986. *(Northamptonshire Police Museum)*

In 1981, a 150th Anniversary Parade was held for the Northamptonshire Police Special Constabulary. The parade was held on the Market Square, Northampton, and all divisions of the county were represented. *(Northamptonshire Police Museum)*

The parade was inspected by the Lord Lieutenant of Northamptonshire, Lieutenant-Colonel John Chandos-Pole, accompanied by Eric Osbourne (on the extreme left), the Commandant of C Division (Northampton) of the Special Constabulary and Deputy Chief Constable Lancelot Scarth. The Lord Lieutenant is just about to talk to Special Constable Cyril Carroll, who was stationed at Oundle. *(Northamptonshire Police Museum)*

Even HM the Queen has time for traffic wardens, which, because they deal with traffic, are under police control. Traffic warden Jim Neish is seen here chatting to the Queen while she was on a visit to Corby in 1982. *(Northamptonshire Police Museum)*

The force switched to Ford patrol cars after the BLMC 2200s were phased out. This is one of the first, seen here in 1982. *(Northamptonshire Police Museum)*

Left: The new extensions to Wootton Hall were officially opened by HRH the Princess Royal on 3 November 1983. *(Northamptonshire Police Museum)*

Below: Chief Constable Maurice Buck looks on while the Princess signs the Visitors' Book. *(Northamptonshire Police Museum)*

Opposite above: The Roger Flawn Cup was given by his parents in memory of PC Roger Flawn, a probationer constable of the force who was killed while driving home from night duty. The cup is given for the most outstanding probationer constable (the first two years of service) of the year. This is WPC Jacqui Squires winning the cup in 1983. *(Northamptonshire Police Museum)*

Regular crime prevention competitions were held in the 1980s for schoolchildren – today's term is 'outreach' – from over the whole of the county. This presentation of prizes in 1985 was by the Deputy Chief Constable, Ivan Forder, at Wellingborough. Looking over his shoulder is Phil Ingram, Superintendent of the Wellingborough Division. After retirement from Northamptonshire Police, Mr Ingram was appointed Chief Constable of the Sovereign Base Areas Police in Cyprus, which polices the two British military enclaves on the island: Dhekalia Garrison, near to Larnaca, and RAF Akrotiri/Episkopi, near Limassol. *(Northamptonshire Police Museum)*

The Spencer family has been at the forefront of Northamptonshire life for several hundred years. This is HRH the Princess of Wales opening Spencer House, an acute admissions unit at St Andrew's Hospital in Northampton, in July 1983. *(Northamptonshire Police Museum)*

As with the 1926 General Strike, the Miners' Strike of March 1984 to March 1985 necessitated sending squads of men away for weeks at a time to the northern coalfields. The Welbeck Colliery is in Nottinghamshire. *(Northamptonshire Police Museum)*

Possibly one of the last times the Marquess of Northampton's First Aid Cup was competed for – this is the victorious team in 1985, now consisting of a mixed team rather than all male. WPC Allison Setchell (left) and WPC Jacqui Squiers, PC Nigel Labrum and Detective Inspector Roger Bonham proudly show off their trophy. DI Roger Bonham also has a place in history as the very last police constable to join the old Northampton Borough Police, being sworn in on 28 March 1966; just three days before the force ceased to exist. *(Northamptonshire Police Museum)*

Due to the number of incidents which occurred off the beaten track, a mobile police station/incident control vehicle was acquired. It was fully equipped with all the obvious things – including radio and tea-making facilities – that were required at an incident in the middle of nowhere. Because it was such a heavy and lumbering vehicle to drive, it quickly became nicknamed 'Miss Piggy' after a character from a well-known television show of the time. *(Northamptonshire Police Museum)*

David O'Dowd joined the Leicester City Police in 1961, reaching the rank of Chief Inspector. In 1977, on promotion to Superintendent, he transferred to West Midlands Police before becoming Assistant Chief Constable of Northamptonshire Police between 1982 and 1984. Two years as Deputy Assistant Commissioner in the Metropolitan Police followed, before he was appointed Chief Constable of Northamptonshire in 1986. He became an Inspector of Constabulary in 1993, and Chief Inspector of Constabulary in 1996, when he was knighted. He retired in 2001. *(Northamptonshire Police Museum)*

ISSUE ONE

NENE BEAT

MAY 1988

MAKING HISTORY

I AM delighted that after some years of discussion, and many months of detailed planning, this newspaper has finally been launched, writes **Chief Constable David O'Dowd.**

The importance of good channels of communication within the force has long been recognised and the launch of **NENE BEAT** is a significant step in the development of the force.

I wish it every success and hope you will all come to regard it, not as a headquarters policy document, but as a key means of keeping you fully informed of what is going on.

It is our newspaper. With your help and contributions it will grow and develop into a constructive link between our extended police 'family'. This includes not only police and civilian staff, but the Specials, members of the Police Authority, retired officers and our own personal families and friends.

● *The Chief, pictured informally at home with his wife Carole and the dogs by DC Barry Holland.*

Munch bunch

MULE TRAINED

The first issue - May 1988

The idea of a newspaper for the force was first put forward in late 1987. A steering committee was formed and the result was *Nene Beat*. This is the front page of the first edition, in May 1988. *Nene Beat* is still going strong, and is distributed to all active and retired members of the force, both police and civilian. Incidentally, the word Nene rhymes with the word 'ten', and not 'been'. *(Northamptonshire Police Museum)*

All Saints' Church,
Northampton

SERVICE OF THANKSGIVING

TO MARK THE

150th ANNIVERSARY OF THE

NORTHAMPTONSHIRE POLICE

EIGHTEEN FORTY~ NINETEEN NINETY
1840~1990

NORTHAMPTONSHIRE
POLICE

Wednesday, 25th April 1990
11 a.m.

The Northamptonshire County Constabulary had been established in 1840. Thus it was deemed that 1990 was the 150th anniversary of the Northamptonshire Police. To celebrate this, the force was granted the Freedom of the Borough of Northampton, and numerous events were organised. This is the front cover of the programme for the Service of Thanksgiving, which was held at All Saints Church. *(Northamptonshire Police Museum)*

The Service of Thanksgiving was followed by a march past to the Guildhall to receive the Freedom of the Borough. This is believed to be the only time that a police force has been granted this honour. To commemorate the event, a badge of the arms of the Borough of Northampton is now worn on the left cuff of all Northamptonshire Police uniforms. *(Northamptonshire Police Museum)*

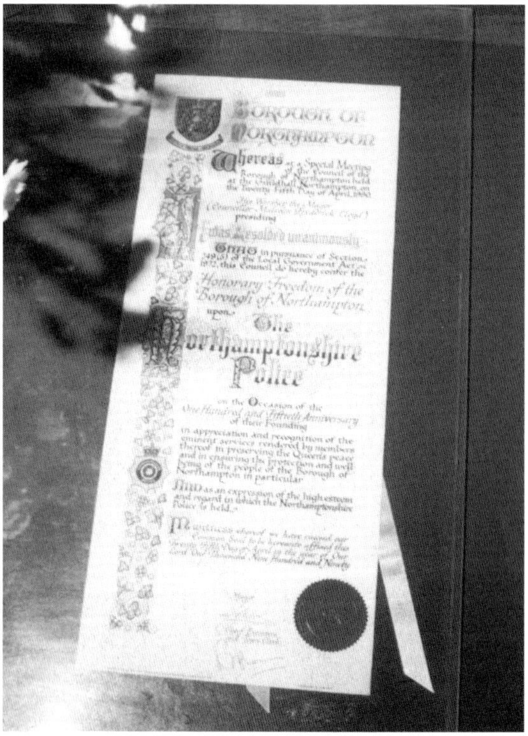

Above: The salute in front of the dais, in front of the Chief Constable, Mr David O'Dowd, and the Mayor of Northampton. Sir Geoffrey Dear, HM Inspector of Constabulary, is seen behind on the right, as well as the Aldermen of the Borough of Northampton on the balcony. *(Northamptonshire Police Museum)*

Left: The Scroll of The Freedom of the Borough, which is kept in a silver casket. Both are now in the Police Museum at Wootton Hall. *(Northamptonshire Police Museum)*

Above: To celebrate the 150th anniversary of the Northamptonshire Police, an exhibition was held at Wootton Hall. The event was well attended by members of the public. These two young men are being shown a Range Rover, which were used as motorway patrol vehicles at the time. The young lady is obviously not mechanically minded. *(Northamptonshire Police Museum)*

Right: Inside the exhibition. On the table nearest the camera are two birches which were used to inflict corporal punishment on offenders, some as young as 12. This practice stopped in 1948. *(Northamptonshire Police Museum)*

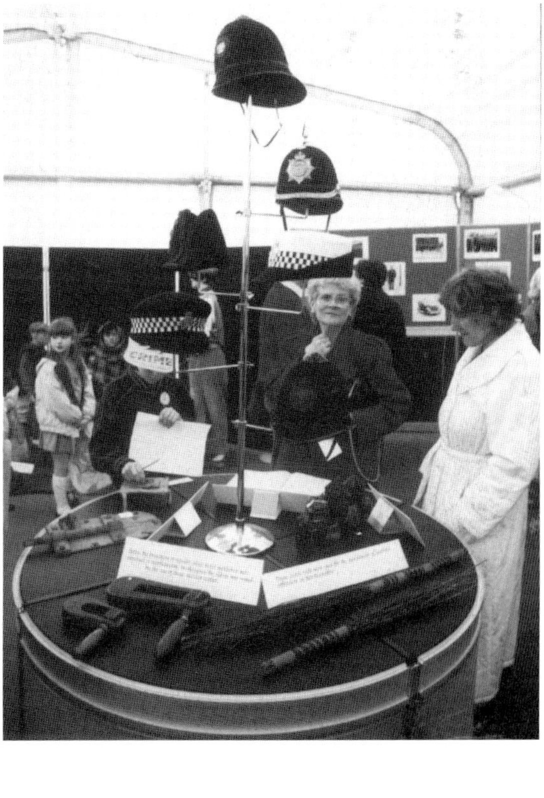

Alongside the exhibition was a 'Children's Party', with all the usual games, recreations and sideshows, including this one, which attracted a disproportionate amount of interest for some reason. The name of the unfortunate 'Bobby' is known, but after some nifty financial negotiations, the author has been sworn to secrecy. *(Northamptonshire Police Museum)*

Edward Crew succeeded David O'Dowd in 1993. He was appointed Chief Constable of the West Midlands Police in 1996, and was knighted in the New Year's Honours of 2001. He retired in 2002. *(Northamptonshire Police Museum)*

National Championships for police dogs and their handlers are held annually. In 1994, Northamptonshire Police Dog Chad was the National Champion. This is our hero posing with his trophies. Also seen here, from left to right are: Sergeant Les Allday, Dog Section Sergeant; Chief Constable Edward Crew; PC Steve Eaton, Chad's handler; Acting Chief Superintendent Trevor Finch. Police Sergeant Allday (along with PS M. Edge, PC J. Grun and PC B. Mitchell) were also in the British Police Unit to Rhodesia during February and March 1980, which assisted in the monitoring of the Rhodesian elections. *(Northamptonshire Police Museum)*

Unfortunately, gun crime is a great problem, and some police officers (not all) have to bear arms at some point. Rigorous training is given, including how to deploy weapons from a motor vehicle, as seen here. Note the car's identification number on the roof so that aerial recognition is made easier. *(Northamptonshire Police Museum)*

Christopher Fox was appointed Chief Constable in 1996. In 2003 he became the Chairman of the Association of Chief Police officers. He was knighted in 2004. *(Northamptonshire Police Museum)*

With the advent of Mr Fox came a brand new badge. Gone is the 'sunburst' pattern with the Northamptonshire Rose and Queen's Crown; being replaced with the badge now in use. Mr Richard Bucknall, Property Services Manager, shows off the new sign intended to replace the old signs and blue lamps outside the county's police stations. *(Northamptonshire Police Museum)*

During the 1990s, Inspector Peter Boatman was a nationally acclaimed teacher of unarmed combat and defensive skills. This photograph shows him on the receiving end from WPC Jacqueline Dimmock. He was awarded the Queen's Police Medal in the New Year's Honours of 1998. *(Northamptonshire Police Museum)*

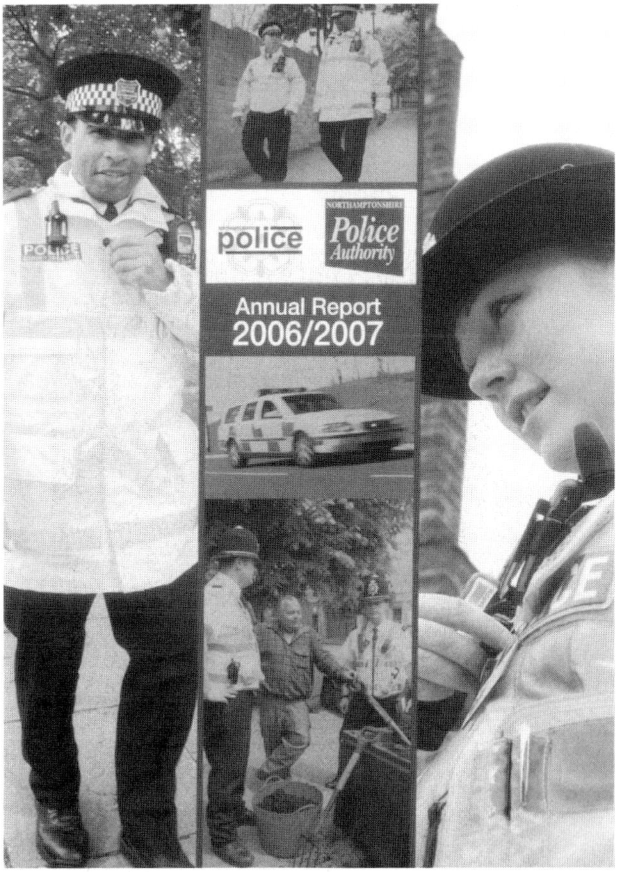

The Annual Reports of the Northampton Borough Police had been printed for public circulation since 1887, when Frederick Mardlin became Chief Constable. The County Constabulary, however, did no such thing, and before 1888 Annual Reports were given only to the Quarter Sessions, and thereafter only to the Standing Joint Committee. It was not until 1944, an incredible 104 years after it first started, that the Northamptonshire County Constabulary printed its Annual Reports for public distribution. Nowadays, of course, Annual Reports are extravagant publications, and are available in all county libraries to anyone who cares to consult them. *(Northamptonshire Police Museum)*

A modern patrol vehicle on the M1 motorway, painted in the 'Battenburg' livery. Contrast this with the plain black patrol cars of just thirty years ago, and the white cars of just a few years later. *(Northamptonshire Police Museum)*

Along with Leicestershire Constabulary and Warwickshire Police, Northamptonshire Police share a helicopter for search purposes. The helicopter is stationed at Husbands Bosworth, which is geographically in the middle of all three counties. The pilot is a non-police officer, but the observer is a police officer of the force where the helicopter is working at the time. *(Northamptonshire Police Museum)*

Realising that police officers also need some kind of spiritual direction, as well as just having someone to talk to, to provide that emotional safety valve, the force now has a team of chaplains of various denominations. Standing, from left to right: Danny Conibere, Charlie Nobbs, Alan Jenkins, Paul Welch. Seated, from left to right: Elaine Roberts, Derek Laverty, Jo Williams. *(Northamptonshire Police Museum)*

And what of the future? Fortunately, enough young men and women put themselves forward to become police officers. These officers are some of a recent intake, who must pass two years of probationary training before being accepted as fully-fledged police officers. *(Northamptonshire Police Museum)*

ACKNOWLEDGEMENTS

I thank the Chief Constable, Mr Peter Maddison QPM, for permission to trawl the archives and to use anything in it which caught my fancy. I also thank Mrs Pat Percival MBE, Head of Corporate Communications, Northamptonshire Police, for putting up with my many foibles, while at the same time lending a helping hand. My thanks also to Ms Alana Miller in the Force Registry for immutable blitheness, and for keeping my paperwork and messages filed where they should be.

There are many people who helped me, and either gave me their expertise, photographs or memories: Mr David Bailey and Mrs Angela Malin of the Northamptonshire Police; Mr Eric Fowell of Rushden; Mr Peter Holyoak of Corby; Mr Michael Shanahan of Great Oakley; the staff of the Caernarfonshire Record Office; the staff of the Northamptonshire Record Office, especially Miss Juliette Baxter; and Mr Bob Carter of Wellingborough Borough Council. I would like to thank them all. Although I have enjoyed compiling this book, it would have been far harder had I not have had their unstinting support.

Finally I would like to add special thanks to Mr Tom Paintain of Weston Favell, and Mr Graham Rogers of Kettering. It was Tom Paintain who first started the Police Museum and Archive at Wootton Hall many moons ago. It is because of his sheer doggedness in collecting together – and cataloguing – documents, artefacts and photographs that would otherwise have been consigned to a more cryptic fate, that the Police Museum and Archive has the amount of material that it does today. His total urbanity whenever I bother him with questions never ceases to amaze me, and his award of the British Empire Medal in the New Year's Honours of 1993, for his work in the Police Museum, was well deserved.

Retired Police Inspector Graham Rogers took over as Curator and Archivist from Tom Paintain, and carried on his work collecting documents and photographs. It was Graham's continuation of Tom's work which made it easier for me, when I took over from him, to compile this book. To both of them, I offer my thanks.